W9-BUT-415

Pleasures and Pains

A Theory of Qualitative Hedonism

By the same author

Freedom, Responsibility, and Obligation

*Reason and Religion: An Introduction to
the Philosophy of Religion*

Pleasures and Pains

A Theory of Qualitative Hedonism

REM B. EDWARDS

Cornell University Press ITHACA AND LONDON

In the spirit of Robert S. Hartman

Contents

7

Preface

So far as I know, this book is the only sustained attempt to make sense out of John Stuart Mill's claim that pleasures and pains differ qualitatively as well as quantitatively, and to explore the ethical applications and ramifications of this claim. Although almost every undergraduate course in ethics deals with the concept of intrinsic goodness and badness and with hedonistic and nonhedonistic answers to the question of what is intrinsically good or evil, almost every available ethics textbook assumes that purely quantitative hedonism is the only viable form of the theory and dismisses Mill's qualitative hedonism as nonsense. It is Mill's theory of action, not his theory of qualitative hedonism, to which most contemporary philosophers give their attention. The latter theory lies just about where Mill left it more than a century ago.

Yet qualitative hedonism should be of utmost interest to anyone who is ready to ask the questions of what life means and under what conditions, if any, life ceases to be worth perpetuating—for the answers it provides are among the most highly plausible ever developed. The theory assumes that the meaning of life is to be found in the intrinsic goodness of the enjoyment of certain activities and experiences which life makes possible. It assumes that the meaning of life is intrinsic to life itself, for the happy life as qualitative hedonism conceives it is an end in itself and does not derive its worth from anything else, including God and immortality.

The theory does not, of course, rule out belief in either one, but it does to some extent consider both in terms of the primary and independent value of human happiness. We might find it objectionable to think of God as "a celestial Jeremy Bentham," as C. D. Broad once suggested; but if we understand John Stuart Mill properly it is not objectionable to think of God as a celestial Mill, whose benevolence consists precisely in his willing the highest possible forms of happiness for all his creatures. Moreover, the very idea of a desirable or meaningful immortality presupposes an intelligible answer to the question of what makes life worthwhile. If there is survival after death, it could very well be as empty and pointless as the inane, gloomy, shadowy, semiconscious existence of the ancient Hebrew *sheol* and the underworld of the Homeric Greeks. And what could have less inherent worth than immortality in a traditional Christian hell? Since immortality itself may be meaningless, it cannot supply an answer to the question of life's meaning. Unless at least some of the concrete experiences and activities of living are inherently valuable, neither this life nor any other can possibly have any innate significance.

Modern medical technology now makes possible the indefinite prolongation of minimal biological survival in a totally and irreversibly comatose state, forcing us to ask ourselves whether life ever ceases to be worth perpetuating. Qualitative hedonism provides a clear response. Where there is no hope of consciousness, the point of living disappears, for happiness presupposes consciousness. Even when consciousness is present, if excruciating and unrelievable pain overwhelmingly predominates, the perpetuation of life may well become an act of cruelty rather than kindness. Of course we should not opt too hastily for death in such cases, but it is also obvious that quality-of-life considerations are relevant to our reflections on dying as well as on living.

Philosophers and nonphilosophers have offered many replies to the question of the nature of the intrinsic goodness of life, or the lack thereof. This book is organized to facilitate the search for a reasonable answer. In the first chapter, the major options of traditional quantitative hedonism, qualitative hedonism, and nonhedonistic pluralism are introduced. Alternatives to qualitative hedonism have been thoroughly explained by other philosophers, but qualitative hedonism itself has never been well developed or understood. The second chapter attempts to remedy this defect by presenting a detailed and experientially applicable analysis of Mill's unexplained contention that pleasures (and pains) differ qualitatively as well as quantitatively. Although some of the more subtle features of a theory of qualitative hedonism remain to be developed in later chapters, enough is understood at the end of Chapter 2 for an intelligible contrast with quantitative hedonism to be presented in Chapter 3. There a new critique of the latter is given, showing its conceptual, psychological, and ethical inadequacies, and explaining why qualitative hedonism is not committed to its embarrassing implications. In Chapter 4, the essential features of a system of qualitative hedonism are expounded, and we see how they have been anticipated historically by many philosophers. After exploring the question of the intentionality of pleasures and pains in this chapter, we are ready to contrast qualitative hedonism with pluralistic views of intrinsic good and bad in Chapter 5. Here we also confront the topics of ranking pleasures and pains, of the nature of happiness and the good life, and of the relation of qualitative hedonism to theories of moral action and obligation. In the final chapter, we face up to the fact that we cannot solve the problem of whether qualitative hedonism provides us with the most reasonable position concerning the nature of inherent worth in living until we have some conception of what reasonableness is and how reason actually works as applied to questions of value and practice. Having developed a theory of qualitative hedonism, we still need to know whether it is reasonable to adopt it. Chapter 6 provides such knowledge.

I hope that I have succeeded in giving sense to the supposed nonsense of qualitative hedonism. I believe that many professional philosophers and astute novices in philosophy are already vaguely dissatisfied with traditional discussions of hedonism. If this book stimulates interested readers to rethink some of the relevant issues, I will consider it a success. It is written for the layman and the college student as well as for the professional philosopher, and I hope that many professionals will wish to introduce it to their students.

Although I have dedicated the book to the memory of my late senior colleague Robert S. Hartman, I have not meant to imply that it is an application of his formal axiology. Whereas he believed that intrinsic value consists in the number (a nondenumerable infinity) of properties that an entity possesses, I am convinced that value is a question of kind or quality rather than number. I would concede that we can take qualitatively distinct pleasures in individuals, classes, and formal constructs; and to that extent his beliefs and mine might not be so far apart. Despite our profound philosophical differences, which often emerged in discussion and debate, I grew to respect Professor Hartman deeply as a distinguished philosopher and superb teacher. I also came to revere him as a man with a keen sensitivity to human values and the philosophical problems associated with them, and as a brilliant creative thinker dedicated to cutting through the dead crust of tradition that so long has bound us as philosophical axiologists. In this latter respect, I hope and believe that this book was written in his spirit.

I wish to express thanks to my undergraduate and graduate students at the University of Tennessee, who have listened with interest and patience to the presentation of many of the ideas expressed here and have responded with helpful critical and constructive comments. John W. Davis, Glenn Graber, and Richard Aquila of my department have read my manuscript and made a large number of valuable suggestions. The secretarial assistance of Dolores Scates, our departmental secretary, has been indispensable. I am grateful also to the staff of Cornell University Press. To all of these people I give my sincere thanks, and to my wife and two children, who have helped me to find and live a happy life.

A slightly different form of Chapter 2 appeared as an article entitled "Do Pleasures and Pains Differ Qualitatively?" in *The Journal of Value Inquiry,* 9 (1975), 270–281, and I am grateful to the editor for permission to use this material. I also wish to thank many publishers for permission to reprint paraphrase passages from books. Material from Aldous Huxley, *Brave New World and Brave New World Revisited,* copyright 1932, 1946, 1958, 1960, 1965, is used by permission of Harper & Row, Publishers, Mrs. Laura Huxley, and Chatto & Windus, Ltd. Paul W. Taylor's *Normative Discourse,* © 1961, is paraphrased by permission of Prentice-Hall, Inc., Englewood Cliffs, New Jersey. Oxford University Press has allowed me to use quotations from "Ethica Nicomachea" translated by W. D. Ross, from *The Oxford Translation of Aristotle* edited by W. D. Ross, Volume 9, 1925, and from *The Dialogues of Plato,* translated by Benjamin Jowett, 4th edition, 1953. Material from J. J. C. Smart and Bernard Williams, *Utilitarianism, For and Against,* and from G. E. Moore,

Preface

Principia Ethica, is used by permission of Cambridge University Press. Quotations from C. D. Broad's *Five Types of Ethical Theory* appear with permission of Routledge & Kegan Paul, Ltd., and Humanities Press. Excerpts from John Stuart Mill, *Utilitarianism, with Critical Essays,* edited by Samuel Gorovitz, copyright © 1971 by The Bobbs-Merrill Company, Inc., are reprinted by permission.

Rem B. Edwards

Knoxville, Tennessee

Pleasures and Pains

A Theory of Qualitative Hedonism

1

What Is Hedonism?

What in life is really worth living for? This question has ✓
intrigued philosophers and nonphilosophers alike from
time immemorial. It is one thing to know how to make a living,
and another thing altogether to know what makes life worth
living. The latter question is not of purely "academic" interest,
for how a person answers it can make all the difference in the
way he orders his life and activities in the "real world" both
inside and outside the confines of academia. In fact, it may be
the single most important question that a human being can
ever ask or try to answer.

In philosophy, the popular question of what makes life
worth living is subjected to analysis, clarification, and refine-
ment; and it comes out as the question of what things are
intrinsically good. An intrinsic good, by definition, is something worth having, achieving, choosing, desiring, experiencing, bringing into existence, or sustaining in existence, for its
own sake. It is an end in itself and not to be desired or chosen

17

simply as a means to some goal which lies beyond it. An intrinsic bad or evil is something worth avoiding for its own sake. Good things chosen merely as means are extrinsic goods, but intrinsic goods are chosen because of their own inherent or self-contained worth. Some things may be both intrinsically and extrinsically good at the same time. If love, knowledge, and pleasure are intrinsically good, they may also be extrinsically good; for there is a sense in which love may lead to more love, knowledge to more knowledge, and pleasure to more pleasure. But if they are intrinsic goods, none of them can be *merely* a means to an end.

What makes life worth living? This seems to mean: "What is there in life that is worth having, experiencing, choosing, desiring for its own sake?" The question is of almost universal human interest. It is not easily answered and the responses proposed are invariably highly controversial. Hedonism is one such controversial answer. The term is derived from the Greek word *hēdonē*, meaning "pleasure," and hedonism is basically the theory that pleasure is the only intrinsic good. It has been such a fundamental and tenaciously long-lived theory that all the alternatives to it may with some justice be grouped together under the one label of *nonhedonistic* theories. Let us examine more closely what is involved in hedonistic and nonhedonistic views of what is intrinsically good.

The Definition of Hedonism

Although there are psychological versions of hedonism which maintain that the pursuit of pleasure alone or the avoidance of pain alone are the sole activities of which we human beings are capable, our attention in this book will be confined to normative hedonism, which presents the pursuit of pleasure or happiness and the avoidance of pain or unhappiness as *ideals* of action to which there are viable alternatives, rather than as necessities of human nature. Normative hedonism is the theory that:

(1) Pleasure, or happiness defined in terms of pleasure, is the *only* thing which is intrinsically good; and pain, or unhappiness defined in terms of pain, is the *only* thing which is intrinsically evil.

(2) *Happiness,* hedonistically defined, consists of a positive surplus of pleasure over pain through an extended period of time; *unhappiness,* hedonistically defined, consists of a surplus of pain over pleasure through an extended period of time.

(3) I *ought to act* to maximize pleasure or happiness and to minimize pain or unhappiness.[1]

Each of these points needs some explaining.

(1) We are not hedonists merely because we are interested in the pursuit of happiness, or because we regard pleasure or happiness as an intrinsically good thing. To qualify as hedonists, we must be *exclusively* interested in the pursuit of happiness, and must regard pleasure or happiness as the sole intrinsic good. Unless we can accept this stronger claim, we are not hedonists; and if we provide a constructive alternative answer to the question of what is intrinsically good, we are nonhedonists. Nonhedonistic theories may be divided into *antihedonistic* theories and *pluralistic* theories.

Antihedonistic theories assert that pleasure or happiness, hedonistically conceived, are not intrinsically good at all, and that pleasure or happiness should not be pursued. The Greek Cynics and Early Stoics seem to have been antihedonists, though their antihedonism may have rested upon a confusion about the meaning of the word "pleasure" which only qualitative hedonism can clarify, that is, a confusion of "lower" with "higher" qualities of pleasure. The Stoics seemed to want to throw out the latter with the former because the same word "pleasure" covered both. Antisthenes the Cynic is supposed to

19

have said that he would rather go mad than experience the first drop of pleasure. Cleanthes, one of the Early Stoics, taught that all pleasure was contrary to nature, including the pleasures of moral virtue. He suggested that to experience pleasure was the worst thing that could happen to a man. For both the Cynics and the Early Stoics, the good life for man consisted in the development and exercise of virtue and reason, and all enjoyment, insofar as this involved agreeable feeling, was to be avoided altogether. Even virtue and reason were ideally to be exercised without enjoyment. Antihedonism is represented in modern philosophy in the writings of Friedrich Nietzsche, as typified by his remark that "Man does *not* strive for pleasure; only the Englishman does."[2]

Most nonhedonists have not been antihedonists, however. *Pluralists* hold that other things besides pleasure are intrinsically good, that more than one thing is intrinsically good. Pluralists concede that pleasure is one among several things worth choosing, pursuing, experiencing, cultivating, and preserving for their own sakes, but they have nominated various other goods as intrinsic goods, among them knowledge, truth, virtue, intimate personal relations, freedom, beauty, and artistic and intellectual creativity. Hedonists and pluralists thus agree that pleasure is *one* good, but they disagree on the question whether it is *the only* good. It is important not to lose sight of the fact that even the pluralist can be interested in the pursuit of happiness as *an* intrinsic good, though he cannot be interested in the pursuit of happiness to the exclusion of all other possible intrinsic goods.

Although some hedonists such as Jeremy Bentham may have subscribed to the theory that "good means pleasant" and "bad means painful," such linguistic theses are not integral to hedonism, and versions of hedonism are available that do not commit what G. E. Moore called the "naturalistic fallacy,"[3] the fallacy of treating "good" as synonymous with "pleasant" or "desired" or some other concept denoting a natural property. Whether the naturalistic fallacy really is a fallacy is of little interest to us here, but we should point out that hedonism does not stand or fall with such naturalistic definitions of "good." If we decide that Moore was right in holding that "what does 'good' *mean?*" and "what *things* are good?" are two entirely different questions requiring entirely different answers, hedonism may still be presented and defended as a highly plausible answer to the second question, and was so treated by Henry Sidgwick. Although "good" may not mean "pleasant," it may still be the case that pleasure is *the only thing* in the world to which the concept of intrinsic good ever legitimately applies.

(2) Hedonistically conceived, "happiness" consists in a positive surplus of pleasure over pain (ideally no pain at all) over an extended period of time. Particular pleasures are the ingredients of happiness; take them away and there is no happiness at all. It would be awkward to say, "I was happy for five seconds," and less awkward to say "I experienced pleasure for five seconds." The difference between happiness and pleasure is the element of time—five seconds is just not long enough for happiness, though a day, week, month, or season might be. Where between five seconds and a day is the line to be drawn? There is no exact answer to the question of "how long" pleasures must prevail if we are to speak of happiness rather than pleasure, just as there is no exact answer in terms of minutes or even years to the question as to when the Middle Ages began and ended, but vague concepts are often just what we need.

There is no exact answer to the question of how intense or prolonged pleasures must be in order to compose a positive surplus of pleasure over pain. And the same sort of indefiniteness about duration and intensity is involved in the hedonistic concept of unhappiness, which consists of a surplus of pain or disagreeable feeling over pleasure, at worst no pleasure at all, over an extended period of time. It is appropriate to call ourselves happy in the hedonistic sense if our agreeable feeling ranges anywhere from a minimal positive balance of contentment with our lot to unspeakable ecstasy. When the balance is tipped in favor of disagreeable feeling, unhappiness is the appropriate word for our state of mind. But the point at which the balance is tipped is exceedingly variable from person to person and from time to time for any given person. John Stuart Mill called attention to this sort of variability and the corresponding indefiniteness in the hedonistic concept of happiness:

> The main constituents of a satisfied life appear to be two, either of which by itself is often found sufficient for the purpose: tranquility and excitement. With much tranquility, many find that they can be content with very little pleasure; with much excitement, many can reconcile themselves to a considerable quantity of pain. There is assuredly no inherent impossibility of enabling even the mass of mankind to unite both, since the two are so far from being incompatible that they are in natural alliance, the prolongation of either being a preparation for, and exciting a wish for, the other. It is only those in whom indolence amounts to a vice that do not desire excitement after an interval of repose; it is only those in whom the need of excitement is a disease that feel the tranquility which follows excitement dull and insipid, instead of pleasurable in direct proportion to the excitement which preceded it.[4]

In qualitative hedonism, the inherent indefiniteness of the notion of "positive surplus" is further complicated by the fact that pleasures and pains differ in qualitative superiority and inferiority as well as in such quantitative ways as intensity and duration. In defining "hedonism," concepts of pleasure and pain should not be understood so narrowly that only quantitative hedonism qualifies.

The hedonist is not committed to the thesis that his definition of "happiness" is the definition that prevails in "ordinary language," though he may believe incidentally that it is at least one of our "ordinary-language" meanings. He is offering us a complete theoretical answer to the question of what is intrinsically good or bad rather than an interesting bit of lexicography. Everything hedonists regard as intrinsically good must be included in the hedonistic definition of "happiness," and everything they regard as intrinsically bad must be included in that of "unhappiness."

(3) All forms of hedonism seem to have an imperative or deontological element. Every hedonist advocates the active pursuit of happiness and the avoidance of unhappiness. But hedonism as such is neutral on the questions of for whom this happiness should be achieved and when it should be enjoyed. I should act to maximize happiness and minimize unhappiness, but for whom? To get an answer to this question, hedonism must be combined with other theories of action that try to answer questions of value distribution, such as egoism, universalism, racism, or nationalism. All such theories may be viewed profitably as attempts to answer the question of how we should act to distribute intrinsic value. Egoism says act to distribute it only to oneself. Universalism says act to distribute it to everyone, or, as John Stuart Mill put it, to "the whole sentient creation."[5] Racism says to distribute it only to members of a favored race, nationalism only to members of a favored nation, and so on. But there may be hedonistic and nonhedonistic forms of egoism, universalism, racism, and nationalism, depending on how the question of what things are intrinsically good is answered.

Special care should be taken to distinguish hedonism from egoism. The two are popularly confused; "hedonist" and "egoist" are often treated as synonyms in everyday moralizing. Yet, hedonism and egoism are answers to two entirely different questions: What things are intrinsically good? and How should I act to distribute intrinsic goods? The egoist holds that he should act to distribute the good things of life, whatever they are, only to himself; but he may give a pluralistic or a hedonistic answer to the question of what they are. The hedonist holds that only pleasure or happiness is intrinsically good, but he may give either an egoistic or a nonegoistic answer to the question of how it should be distributed. In the arena of distribution, the happiness or welfare of me alone lies at one extreme, and the greatest happiness or welfare of the greatest possible number of persons or sentient beings lies at the other. In between lies the happiness or welfare of the members of a race or nation or the like. Jeremy Bentham seems to have been an egoist,[6] but there are moral or universalistic as well as egoistic forms of hedonism, and other nineteenth-century utilitarians including John Stuart Mill and Henry Sidgwick were universalistic hedonists. The realm of the moral is understood by universalistic utilitarians as pertaining to the advantage or welfare of everyone alike or the greatest possible number of persons or sentient beings. If we decide to be hedonists, we do not thereby decide to be (or not to be) egoists, and the reverse is equally true. The two positions are clearly separate and distinct.

Hedonism as such is thus neutral on the question of "for whom" happiness should be sought, egoistic hedonists giving one reply, universalistic hedonists another, and racistic and nationalistic hedonists still others. Many answers are also possible to the question of *when* this maximum of pleasure is to be pursued and experienced, the basic division here being between the hedonists of the present moment, such as the Greek philosopher Aristippus, who say: "Act to maximize pleasure *now* and don't worry about the future," and the hedonists of the long run, such as Epicurus, who say: "Act to maximize pleasure over the entire span of your life." The latter is a reflective and calculating form of hedonism, and the former is neither. To succeed as a long-run hedonist, it is necessary to know a great deal about what causes what in the world and in the realm of human experience. Some pleasures lead to a predominance of pain over pleasure in the long run, and they are to be avoided; other pleasures lead to future enjoyments of like kind and should be cultivated. To identify the acceptable and unacceptable pleasures, we must know a great deal about what causes people in general to enjoy themselves and to suffer. We also need to know what causes us as individuals to enjoy ourselves and to suffer. The successful hedonist of the long run must have a deep knowledge of the general psychology of human nature, and he must also know himself, since it is often the case that one man's pleasure is another man's poison, or to speak more precisely, that what is a source of pleasure for one man is a source of pain for another.

Most philosophical hedonists have been long-range hedonists, and we shall be interested primarily in long-range hedonism in this book. But a couple of remarks need to be made about short-range hedonism. In the first place, we do learn after a while that the future does not just go away simply because we choose to ignore it. "Eat, drink, and be merry, for tomorrow we die," and "Have a blast while you last" may be acceptable philosophies for those who are reasonably certain that they are not going to last very long, that tomorrow they are going to die. But in the absence of such assurance, most of us would be well advised to order our lives and activities in ways that will probably succeed in maximizing pleasure and minimizing pain over the long haul. In the second place, there is an interesting ambiguity in the notion of "the present moment." How long is it? If "the present moment" is very strictly construed to include only the thin knife-edge of the instant at hand, then hedonism of the present moment cannot be a theory of action at all. It cannot say "Act to maximize pleasure in the *present* moment," for all action aims at *future* results, even if these results lie only a few seconds away. "The present moment" usually means "the next few hours." Don't worry about

the chances of hangover or pregnancy; just live it up tonight—
that is, during the next few hours, if the night is still young. But
if the night is still young, then most of it still lies in the
future; and the real difference between "present-moment" and
"long-run" hedonism lies in the question of *how much* of the
future to consider rather than whether to consider the future
at all. Long-run hedonism does not say that we should act to
maximize merely *future* pleasures, but pleasures over the whole
span of life, which includes the present and immediate future
as well as the distant future. In a sense, the future never comes;
and any philosophy that advocates the actualization of merely
distant future pleasures requires a continual postponement of
enjoyment for the sake of that future which never comes.
Long-run hedonism includes, rather than excludes, present
and immediately future enjoyment, however, since its ideal is
that of happiness over the *entire* span of life.

The Meaning of "Pleasure" and "Pain"

How are pleasure and pain to be identified, as the hedonist
understands them? When we are dealing with words like "pleasure" and "pain," it appears that certain normally applicable
techniques of definition cannot be used. Pleasures and pains
are not sense-objects in the "external" world, and the meaning
of "pleasure" and "pain" cannot be communicated ostensively.
We cannot hold up or point directly to instances of pleasure
and pain and say "Here is one six inches long," "Here is one
that weighs eight ounces," or "Here is one that is bright red, or
dark blue." Nor can pleasure and pain, as the hedonist understands them, be defined in purely behaviorist terms, though
many influential attempts to do this have been made in recent
years. "Pain behavior" and "pleasure behavior" may be criteria
for the correct or incorrect applications of judgment about
pain and pleasure to other minds; but the hedonist is *not* main-

taining that overt, publicly observable, behavioristically testable manifestations of pain and pleasure are intrinsically bad or good. In saying that the pain of a toothache is undesirable in and of itself, the hedonist is not taking the position that such pain behavior as holding my jaw, drying, wincing, or pill-swallowing is bad intrinsically. In saying that the enjoyment of nature is intrinsically good, the hedonist is not asserting that merely standing on the seashore with one's eyes open in the direction of a glorious sunset with no feeling at all is intrinsically good. The pleasure and pain in which the hedonist is interested are inner qualities of feeling, and some small introspective ability is required in order to focus attention upon pleasures and pains in the relevant sense. If introspective psychology is thrown out completely, then hedonism in its classical sense is thrown out with it. Pleasure and pain, as intrinsically desirable or undesirable, have been thought of as inner qualities of feeling or awareness, private feelings which we would naturally like to perpetuate or avoid. Pain is not "pain behavior"; it is the quality of inner feeling that prompts us to behave that way, and the same may be said of pleasure. If all sentient beings are eliminated from our solar system, as we may have the power to do with our chemical, biological, or atomic weaponry, the solar system that remains will have no intrinsic value in it. If the thought is any consolation, it will have no intrinsic disvalue in it either. Its value will be entirely neutral without the presence of sentient beings capable of some measure of awareness of those agreeable feelings we call pleasures and those disagreeable feelings we call pains. The actualization of intrinsic goods and ills as the hedonist identifies them is thus parasitic for its mode of existence upon the presence of sentience or awareness in the world. To put it another way, to the hedonist, no "material object" in the popular sense of external object of sense experience is intrinsically good, though such objects may be extrinsically good as sources of agreeable feel-

27

ing. Thus the hedonist does and must reject three theses of Watsonian metaphysical behaviorism.[7] He cannot accept the claims: (1) that inner awareness or consciousness does not exist, for pleasure and pain as he understands them are qualities of inner awareness and not publicly observable sense-objects or patterns of behavior; (2) that introspection is a totally unreliable and unacceptable source of knowledge, for he must rely upon his own abilities to focus his attention upon his own feelings to tell whether he is experiencing pleasure or pain; and (3) that the words "pleasure" and "pain" can be redefined without loss of sense to be *identical* in meaning with such publicly observable patterns of "pain behavior" as crying, frowning, grimacing, and holding one's side, or such patterns of "pleasure behavior" as smiling and laughing, for it is the inner feelings that may accompany and usually cause such behavior which interest him and which he regards as intrinsically bad or good.

If pleasure and pain cannot be defined ostensively or behavioristically, and if this is true also of all synonyms and roughly equivalent phrases, then how can the meaning of "pleasure" and "pain" as the hedonist understands them be communicated to someone who at least professes to be left in the dark when the hedonist uses the terms? We could not directly point to examples of such entities, as we might if we were teaching the meaning of "yellow" and "green." But we might be able to use an indirect way of combined pointing and speaking. Assuming a kind of common "human nature," we would suggest that our subject try to remember circumstances in which people typically experience pleasure or pain, and that he try to focus his attention on his own remembered feelings in such circumstances. Those feelings that he liked and wanted to sustain, cultivate, repeat would be pleasures; and those feelings that he disliked and wanted to terminate and avoid would be pains. We might approach the problem more directly and try

28

to generate present circumstances that typically cause pleasure or pain, then ask him to focus on any feelings he might wish to sustain or be rid of. A jab with a pin, or a pinch, or a bee sting will typically generate pain. A back rub or sexual stimulation will typically generate pleasure. In such circumstances, if attention is focused on feelings to be eliminated and avoided, or feelings to be sustained and cultivated, then examples of pains and pleasures have been located experientially, and the denotative meaning of these terms has been experientially learned. The assumption of a common human nature that such techniques of communication require is not as doubtful as it appears to be on the surface. Certainly there are many individual and cultural variations in our sources of enjoyment and frustration, but it is also true that a few sources of the same are almost universally human. After all, the person who designs a torture chamber or a weapon of war usually does not have to consider cultural and personal idiosyncrasies to achieve remarkably efficient instruments of suffering and death.

We shall give much more attention to the question of the relation that pleasures and pains have to their sources as our discussion proceeds in later chapters. But now we must turn to the question of whether all pleasures, as pleasures, are the same, and whether all pains, as pains, are the same.

2

Do Pleasures Differ Qualitatively?

Most traditional hedonists such as Epicurus, Bentham, and Sidgwick have been quantitative hedonists, but Francis Hutcheson and John Stuart Mill introduced an interesting complication into the modern theory of hedonism by insisting that pleasures differ qualitatively as well as quantitatively. What does it mean to say that pleasures differ qualitatively? This question has never been answered satisfactorily. To consider it, we must first have a few things about quantitative hedonism clearly in mind.

Hedonism is the theory that only pleasure or happiness defined in terms of pleasure is intrinsically good, and that only pain or unhappiness defined in terms of pain is intrinsically bad. Pleasures and pains are qualities of private inner experience rather than of public sense-objects, but we all presumably have the capacity for experiencing pleasures and pains. As qualities of individual experience, pleasures differ from pains,

30

obviously; and according to the quantitative hedonist pleasures (and pains) may differ among themselves in quantitative ways, in temporal proximity or remoteness, and in causal connections. A given pleasure may differ intrinsically from some other given pleasure, and a given pain from some other given pain, in such quantitative ways as duration and intensity. They may also differ temporally with respect to nearness or remoteness in time. And they may differ extrinsically in their causal connections, one pleasure or pain being causally more probable or certain than another, one tending causally to reproduce its kind purely or as mixed with its opposite.

Traditional hedonists have attempted to distinguish between the "higher pleasures" and the "lower pleasures." Food, drink, and sex are standard examples of the lower pleasures, and the higher pleasures are such things as knowledge, intellectual creativity, art, aesthetic creativity, and intimate personal relations such as friendship. Mill would have agreed with the quantitative hedonists with respect to this classification and its hard-core instances. He would also have agreed with them that, strictly speaking, the instances mentioned are not pleasures, that is, agreeable feelings, at all; they are standard *sources* of pleasure. Some of them may also be classified as sense-objects, others as activities or experiences. The so-called "higher pleasures" listed are actually "higher sources of pleasure," and the "lower pleasures" mentioned are really "lower sources of pleasure." Quantitative hedonists have attempted to explain in strictly quantitative or causal terms why some sources of agreeable feeling are higher and some lower than others. The higher sources are thus said to give longer lasting or more intense pleasures, or they are purer and more fertile in their long-range consequences than the lower sources. Whether this is true is, of course, a highly debatable matter, though we shall not enter upon that debate.

Mill's Account of Qualitative Differences

In saying that pleasures (and presumably also pains) differ qualitatively as well as quantitatively, Mill was saying that one pleasure (or pain) may differ from another not only with respect to its intensity, duration, and causal connections, but also *as a quality of feeling*. Not only are there higher and lower *sources* of agreeable feeling, but there are also higher and lower *pleasures as pleasures,* if Mill is correct. In other words, the quality of agreeable feeling itself which we derive from doing philosophy or hearing a good concert is different from the quality of agreeable feeling which we derive from eating a good meal or from sexual intercourse. In addition to quantitative and causal differences, there are, according to Mill, *two* more ways in which the experienced pleasures differ. They differ psychologically, as qualities of feeling, and also normatively, in desirability. Only when the first psychological point has been established is it appropriate to turn to the second normative point. The qualitative hedonist must thus answer two questions; first, what does it mean to say that pleasures differ in quality? and second, given two qualitatively different pleasures, how are we to determine which is the more desirable? The first of these questions is the one what concerns us in this chapter; it must be distinguished clearly from the second, to which we shall return in Chapter 5.

What then does it mean to say that one pleasure differs in *quality* from another? Mill himself does little to enlighten us on this point. Without attempting to analyze the notion of qualitative differences, he immediately diverts our attention to another problem, our second question of how we tell which of two qualitatively different pleasures is the more desirable. But this presupposes that we have already understood the notion of qualitative differences. Mill does ask the question of meaning.

That he does not answer it but answers our second question instead is perfectly obvious when we look at his remarks:

> If I am asked what I mean by differences of quality in pleasures, or what makes one pleasure more valuable than another, merely as a pleasure, except its being greater in amount, there is but one possible answer. Of two pleasures, if there be one to which all or almost all who have experience of both give a decided preference, irrespective of any feeling of moral obligation to prefer it, that is the most desirable pleasure. If one of the two is, by those who are competently acquainted with both, placed so far above the other that they prefer it, even though knowing it to be attended with a greater amount of discontent, and would not resign it for any quantity of the other pleasure which their nature is capable of, we are justified in ascribing to the preferred enjoyment a superiority in quality so far outweighing quantity as to render it, in comparison, of small account.[1]

Few if any enlightening discussions of the meaning of "qualitative differences in pleasures" have been written since Mill published his *Utilitarianism*. C. D. Broad suggested that Mill "was so confused that he probably did not himself know precisely what he meant"[2] by this expression. Brand Blanshard has recently written, quite correctly, that "higher and lower rank among the qualities of pleasure has proved a most obscure notion."[3]

In the rest of this chapter, I will attempt to give a meaning to the concept of "qualitative differences." Only Mill himself could tell us whether I have "correctly" explicated his enigmatic notion. Nevertheless, the interpretation offered below does seem to me to be a highly plausible one.

First of all, if we momentarily shift the discussion from the realm of psychology into that of linguistics, it seems that Mill might want to say the following things about the words "pleasure" and "pain" (and any synonyms thereof). The quantita-

33

tive hedonist is committed to saying that these words have a univocal denotative meaning or reference. If we speak of the agreeable feeling of sexual arousal and the agreeable feeling of scientific inquiry or discovery as "pleasures," the word "pleasure" means exactly the same thing in both contexts. That is, the referent of the words is a single quality of feeling, though there may be quantitative differences in intensity and duration. The assumption of a single referent for the word "pleasure" doubtless underlies Bentham's remark that "quantity of pleasure being equal, push-pin is as good as poetry." Although Bentham is usually quoted as having put it just this way, what he actually wrote makes it even clearer that he assumed that pleasure is pleasure, no matter how we get it. As he actually phrased it in his *Rationale of Reward,* "Prejudice apart, the game of push-pin is of equal value with the arts and sciences of music and poetry. If the game of push-pin furnish more pleasure, it is more valuable than either. Everybody can play at push-pin: poetry and music are relished only by a few. The game of push-pin is always innocent: it were well could the same be always asserted of poetry."[4] This quote, plus the wider context from which it was abstracted, makes it abundantly clear that John Hospers was quite mistaken in writing that Bentham "was convinced that poetry, in its total effects, direct and indirect, does cause more pleasure than pushpin."[5] Many other interpreters of Bentham make the same mistake. Actually, Bentham believed that pushpin was generally more enjoyable, and thus more valuable, than poetry. He held that more people get more pleasure, unmixed with pain, from pushpin than from poetry; and as a quantitative hedonist he assumed that the quality of pleasure is always the same no matter how it is obtained.

In contrast with Bentham, the qualitative hedonist *should* say that the notions of "pleasure" or "pain" are in a sense ambiguous notions, referring to a wide range of agreeable or disagreeable feelings that are qualitatively distinct. The words have a

variety of referents rather than a single referent, and it is no
simple claim that the hedonist makes when he asserts that only
pleasure is intrinsically good and only pain intrinsically bad.
Ludwig Wittgenstein has shown us that the referents of our
words do not all exhibit common properties but may exemplify
only "family resemblances." In a post-Wittgensteinian age, it
seems exceedingly naive to assume that everything which has a
common name shares a common property, yet this is precisely
the linguistic assumption which has misled the quantitative
hedonists. It was quite explicitly the chief reason given by
Sidgwick in the nineteenth century for rejecting Mill's qualitative hedonism. Sidgwick wrote that "all *qualitative* comparisons
of pleasures must really resolve itself into quantitative. For all
pleasures are understood to be so called because they have a
common property of pleasantness, and may therefore be compared in respect of this common property."[6] Instead of possess-
ing common properties of pleasantness and unpleasantness,
our multifarious "pleasures" and "pains" probably have in
common only that they are feelings which in the former case
we wish to sustain and repeat and in the latter we wish to
eliminate and avoid. "Pleasure" and "pain" are closer to being
"family" concepts than to being "common property" concepts.
In Chapter 4 we shall give a more systematic analysis of them as
concepts.

Now, if we turn back to psychology once more, how can we
distinguish between different kinds of—that is, qualities of—
pleasure and pain? If a meaningful answer can be provided to
this question, qualitative hedonism may after all be saved from
the oblivion to which it is usually consigned.

Localized and Nonlocalized Feelings

In his *Human Conduct,* John Hospers distinguishes between
two different senses of "pleasure" and two different senses of
"pain." I believe that this distinction holds great promise for

illuminating the hitherto obscure concept of qualitative differences in pleasures and pains, though Hospers himself does not develop the distinction in this manner nor in any way relate it to Mill's qualitative hedonism. Hospers calls his two kinds of pleasure "pleasure$_1$" and "pleasure$_2$," the former being nonlocalized agreeable feeling, and the latter localized agreeable feeling. Localized pleasures are those which are given phenomenologically to "raw" experience as being located in some definite part or region of the body, whereas nonlocalized pleasures do not seem to have a precise physical locus but involve a more general sense of well-being. A similar distinction is made among disagreeable feelings. Pains given to immediate experience as being in a definite region of the body are what Hospers calls "pain," though I shall call them "pain$_2$." Hospers does not wish to call the nonlocalized variety of disagreeable feeling "pain." Instead he calls it "displeasure," but I see no serious objection to calling it "pain$_1$." Nonlocalized discomforts have been called "pain" time and time again in the discourse of both philosophers and plain men.

Up to this point, these notions of different kinds of pleasures and pains may seem hardly less obscure than Mill's original notion of "qualitative differences," so let us now explore them in more detail, beginning with the most obvious case, that of localized bodily pains, pain$_2$. These are the kinds of feelings about which we may sensibly ask and answer the doctor's question, "Where does it hurt?" Hospers tells us: "The opposite of pleasure$_2$ is pain. Pain is a sensation, experienced at a definite place; a pain in my tooth, an ache in my side, a stabbing sensation in my big toe. You can sensibly ask, 'Where (in what part of your body) do you feel the pain?'"[7] No special introspective skills are required to identify this kind of disagreeable feeling. All of us except the smallest children can usually understand the doctor who asks us where it hurts, and all of us are familiar with such localized bodily pains as toothache, headache, earache, stomachache, broken bones, burns, bruises, and cuts.

That there is such a thing as localized bodily pleasures might come as a surprise to some people, however. For example, Gilbert Ryle was perfectly willing to recognize localized bodily pains, but explicitly denied the existence of corresponding localized bodily pleasures, pleasure$_2$. "We can tell the doctor where it hurts," he wrote, "and whether it is a throbbing, a stabbing or a burning pain; but we cannot tell him, nor does he ask, where it pleases us, or whether it is a pulsating or a steady pleasure. Most of the questions which can be asked about aches, tickles and other sensations or feelings cannot be asked about our likings and dislikings, our enjoyings and detestings. In a word, pleasure is not a sensation at all, and therefore not a sensation on one scale with an ache or twinge."[8]

In discussing pleasure$_2$, however, Hospers points out, "There are pleasurable sensations, such as those of being tickled, stroked, and rubbed; since these pleasures have a definite bodily location, here it makes sense to ask, '*Where* do you feel the pleasure?'—whereas it does not make sense to ask, 'Where do you feel the pleasure you get from reading a good book?' "[9] Anyone who has ever had his back rubbed or soaked his feet in hot water or been lightly tickled should know that there are localized bodily pleasures, as should anyone who has eaten a good meal and experienced the oral and gastric satisfactions thereof.

Although the existence of localized bodily pleasures does not seem perfectly obvious to Ryle, it does seem obvious to Hospers, and it seems obvious to me. I might add also that it seemed perfectly obvious to Freud and his followers. Although he does not do so, Hospers might profitably have made use of the Freudian concept of "erogenous zones" to explicate further his concept of localized bodily pleasures. In the oral, anal, and genital zones, localized pleasures are *commonly* felt, and in talking about such pleasures it does make sense to ask and answer the question "Where does it feel good?" When we are sexually aroused, for example, we can meaningfully say that it feels

37

good in the genital zones. Ryle is correct, of course, in pointing out that the doctor does not ask us where it pleases us, but this does not imply that we could not tell him. It implies only that we normally do not go in for medical treatment when we are enjoying ourselves. Although it would be socially inappropriate for a doctor to ask us where it felt good, it would not be socially inappropriate for the question to be posed by a masseur or by a sex partner with whom we are engaged in erotic play. Furthermore, the localized pleasure of erotic play is a relatively steady pleasure, though there is no doubt a sense in which it has its ups and downs. By contrast, the localized pleasure of erotic orgasm is a pulsating pleasure. In debating the "merits" of vaginal versus clitoral orgasm in the female, we do ask where it feels good. So Ryle seems to be mistaken on all such counts.

Nonlocalized pleasure$_1$ does, however, fit the pattern developed by Ryle reasonably well. Here questions about location do seem inappropriate, and pleasure does not seem to come as throbbing, stabbing, burning, or pulsating sensations. Since Ryle neglected the point, it needs to be stated that the same may be said for nonlocalized pain$_1$ or displeasure. In discussing nonlocalized pleasure, Hospers writes:

> We may speak of pleasure—let us call it pleasure$_1$—in the sense of a pleasurable state of consciousness, one with "positive hedonic tone." It seems to be impossible to define it further, for the term refers to an experience which, like so many experiences, no words are adequate to describe. We can only cite typical circumstances under which this experience occurs: we may derive this kind of pleasure from such sources as a refreshing swim, from reading a good book, from grappling with a philosophical problem, from creating a work of art, or from talking with congenial persons. Pleasure in this sense is, as Aristotle said, an accompaniment of activity; of course different people experience pleasure and experience it to widely different degrees and from widely varying activities: some people experience pleasure from mathematical pursuits, for example, and others do not. From what-

ever sources it may be derived, pleasure is an accompaniment of an activity, like a frosting on a cake—the frosting tops the cake but is not found by itself apart from the cake.[10]

Other sources of nonlocalized agreeable feeling mentioned by Hospers include "good books, symphony concerts, and doing one's duty" and even "the pleasure of worshipping God."[11] *Where* does it feel good when we are enjoying a good book or a concert? *Where* are the pleasure of mystical rapture located? There seems to be no clear meaning to these questions because these pleasures are not localized in some definite part of the body such as the right side of the abdomen or the back of the head. The localized pleasures of eating a peppermint ice cream cone are clearly concentrated in the oral zone of the body, but the nonlocalized pleasures of hearing a concert are just as clearly *not* concentrated in the auditory zone, though these are the senses which are being stimulated. The pleasures of sight, in which we delight above all other sensory pleasures, as Aristotle noted, are likewise not concentrated in the optic zone.

Nonlocalized pain$_1$, which Hospers prefers to call "displeasure," is said by him to be "not a sensation and thus not locatable, and it makes no sense to ask, 'Where did you feel the pain you experienced at hearing the bad news?'"[12] He further explains that "displeasure would include all unpleasant states of consciousness, such as we experience from bodily pain, from hearing bad news, from situations involving distress, anger, terror, and jealousy."[13] It is of course possible to extend this list to include the affective components of such states of mind as intense grief over the death of a loved one and the "existentialist" moods of dread, despair, melancholy, loneliness, boredom, alienation, disappointment, meaninglessness, and guilt. It should be noticed that nonlocalized feeling is not the same thing as universally localized feeling. The former has no definite bodily locus at all, whereas the latter seems to be present "all over." Fatigue and chill are universally localized discomforts, whereas the pleasures of drunkenness are universally localized comforts. (The taste and gastric pleasures of drinking are regionally localized, but those of drunkenness itself seem to be felt "all over.")

Most of the "sources" or kinds of nonlocalized pleasure$_1$ that Hospers mentioned would appear on traditional lists of the "higher sources of pleasure" and Mill would have termed them "qualitatively superior." Likewise, most kinds of pleasure$_2$ are traditionally "lower sources" and belong in Mill's "qualitatively inferior" category. We shall soon see that the lower pleasures typically generate the higher ones, but it is true that the basic pleasures of food, drink, and sex are localized bodily ones. To be sure, the difference we have developed between sorts of pleasure and pain thus far has been primarily one of *locus,* but once this difference is clearly understood, it is not difficult to see that the agreeable or disagreeable feelings themselves are just not qualitatively the *same* feelings, capable of differing as feelings only in intensity and duration. The agreeable feeling of scientific discovery or philosophical creativity is just not the same *kind* as the agreeable feeling of a back rub or an erotic erection, only different in intensity and duration. The disagreeable feeling of intense grief over the death of a loved one is just not the same *kind* of disagreeable feeling as that of a burn, bee sting, or toothache. We just happen to have an impoverished vocabulary for dealing with the diversity of feelings involved; we need at least as many words for "pleasure" and "pain" as the Eskimos have for "snow." Mill does not develop in much detail a distinction between "qualitatively bad" and "qualitatively worse" pains; but if he had, he doubtless would have maintained that although localized bodily pains are bad enough, they are not as intrinsically undesirable as the qualitatively different and worse nonlocalized disagreeable feelings that are the affective ingredients of fear or terror, anger,

hatred, jealousy, loneliness, boredom, alienation, disappointment, anxiety, dread, despair, melancholy, or guilt. It does
seem clear that there are significant qualitative differences
among pains, that is, disagreeable feelings, just as there are
among pleasures. Seeing that pleasures and pains differ in
locus is not the same as seeing that they differ in quality, but it
is a key that unlocks a previously closed door through which we
may enter to gain new visions of the complexity of human
feelings and of any theory of value that would identify human
feelings as intrinsic goods or intrinsic bads.

Classifying the above mentioned "pains of soul" as nonlocalized does not entail a denial of the fact that they are often
accompanied by localized discomforts. Rollo May has written
that "acute loneliness seems to be the most painful kind of
anxiety which a human being can suffer. Patients often tell us
that the pain is a physical gnawing in their chests, or feels like
the cutting of a razor in their heart region, as well as a mental
state of feeling like an infant abandoned in a world where
nobody exists."[14]

Although John Hospers rejects qualitative hedonism as unintelligible in his short discussion of Mill,[15] he nevertheless makes
a move in his consideration of the hedonistic conception of
"happiness" which a quantitative hedonist who does not recognize differences in quality is not entitled to make.[16] In explicating what he still believes to be a quantitatively hedonistic conception of "happiness," Hospers tells us, "Clearly, it is pleasure$_1$
that is of relevance to ethics, and it is pleasure$_1$ which people
have (however dimly) in mind when they say that pleasure is
intrinsically good."[17] He further suggests that for the hedonist,
"It is pleasures$_1$, not pleasures$_2$, that are the ingredients of
happiness, though of course pleasures$_2$, by causing pleasures$_1$,
may thereby sometimes contribute to happiness."[18]

What must be recognized, however, is that the quantitative
hedonist has no basis whatsoever for discriminating against

41

some pleasures or pains because they are localized. For him, pleasure is pleasure, and pain is pain. Furthermore, as we pointed out in Chapter 1, an adequate hedonistic definition of "happiness" must include *everything* that the hedonist regards as intrinsically good; otherwise happiness plus something else will be intrinsically good, and the hedonist will turn out to be a pluralist! Similarly, the hedonistic concept of "unhappiness" must include everything that the hedonist regards as intrinsically bad. Hospers does not say explicitly that localized bodily pains are excluded from the hedonistic conception of "unhappiness," because he does not discuss "unhappiness" in this context, but, if localized pleasures are excluded from "happiness," logical symmetry would seem to require that localized pains be excluded from "unhappiness." This would be a very strange result, however. If there is anything that *all* hedonists agree upon, it is that prolonged, excruciating bodily pain is an intrinsic evil, to be avoided for its own nasty sake. Unhappiness, in the hedonistic sense, as a complete hedonistic answer to the question of intrinsic evil, will clearly have to include both such nonlocalized discomforts as those of jealousy, grief, guilt, and despair, and also such localized discomforts as the pain of a toothache, a bee sting, or terminal cancer. If this is granted, symmetry, as well as the assumption that "pleasure is pleasure," would seem to require that "happiness" in the quantitatively hedonistic sense must include both localized and nonlocalized pleasures.

Though Hospers's distinction between two types of pleasure and pain is of questionable utility in the attempt to understand the quantitatively hedonistic concepts of "happiness" and "unhappiness," nevertheless it might help us to understand what is meant by the qualitatively hedonistic claims that the lower pleasures are "physical" or "sensory," and the higher pleasures are "mental" or "nonsensory." These expressions are to be found in our popular discussions of hedonism as well as in the writings of such philosophers as Plato and Mill. Yet, this obscure way of contrasting pleasures and pains has seldom if ever been well explained, and there are certain interpretations of these terms which just do not work at all. If by "physical" or "sensory" it is meant that these pleasures result from the stimulation of the "external" senses of touch, taste, hearing, sight, smell, this is often just as true of the "higher" pleasures as of the "lower" ones. The "higher" enjoyment of any of the fine arts involves stimulation of the senses, especially those of sight and hearing. The joys of friendship come from *visible* friends, for most of us at any rate. Then again, if by "physical" it is meant that some bodily, physiological, or neurological processes are components or concomitants of agreeable and disagreeable feeling, this too is presumably just as true of the higher as of the lower pleasures. The distinction which Hospers makes between localized bodily and nonlocalized pleasures and pains would not be at all obviated even if the neurological theory which says that "pleasures and pains are all really in the brain and never in the left arm or right side of the jaw" should turn out to be true. This distinction is independent of neurology, both in the sense that it could be explained to a person who knows so little about anatomy that he does not even know that human beings have brains, and in the sense that it is a phenomenological rather than a neurological distinction. That is, it is based upon how pleasures are given to immediate experience, as localized or nonlocalized, rather than upon a detailed knowledge of anatomy. After all, it is the phenomenology of pleasure and pain that really interests the hedonist, for it is *experienced* pleasure and pain that is good or bad in his view. Nevertheless, neurological processes probably are causes, components, or concomitants (depending on the metaphysics of one's philosophy of mind, of which qualitative hedonism is also independent) of every experience of pleasure or pain, whether it be localized or nonlocalized; and if this is the case, then "mental" pleasure cannot be distinguished from "physical" pleasure on the grounds that the latter involve neurological (physical) processes whereas the former do not. The most meaningful way to explain the distinction between the "mental" and the "physical" seems to be the phenomenological one suggested implicitly by Hospers: the "physical" or "sensory" pleasures and pains are the localized bodily ones, and the "mental" or "nonsensory" ones are the nonlocalized ones.

Traditional quantitative hedonists have always been interested in the causal contexts and consequences of pleasures and pains. If qualitative hedonism is developed along the lines suggested above, new paths of investigation are opened up. It is now possible to explore the causal connections between localized and nonlocalized pleasures and pains, that is, between the higher and lower pleasures and pains. Let me give a few illustrations. Such causal connections need not be immediate in time, and other causal conditions are always presupposed in all such illustrations.

Hospers has done some thinking already about the causal connections between different types of pleasure and pain. He has pointed out that pleasure$_2$ does normally give rise to the generalized feeling of well-being involved in pleasure$_1$, that similar relations usually obtain between localized bodily pain and displeasure, and that the masochist is unusual or abnormal because he obtains pleasure$_1$ from localized pain$_2$.[19] The pleasures of eating, drinking, and sex play frequently lead to a generalized feeling of well-being, and the pains of injury and disease often bring about a generalized sense of depression, despair, or hopelessness about oneself. It is possible to carry this investigation of causal connections far beyond where Hospers left it, however. The localized pleasures of sex do not always give rise to a generalized sense of well-being for everyone, but only in certain contexts. One possible interpretation of the popular saying that "sex without love is meaningless or empty" is that here, for some people, only pleasure$_2$ is generated, not pleasure$_1$. The localized pleasures of sex may also generate the localized pains$_2$ of childbirth or venereal diseases and the nonlocalized pain$_1$ feelings of guilt or possibly even the "mental" discomfort of an unwanted pregnancy. Conversely, the localized pains of birth typically lead to the nonlocalized elation of motherhood. Someone attempting to comfort a child whose pet cat has been run over by an automobile may do so by diverting his mind from the nonlocalized pains of grief by generating localized pleasure$_2$ through stroking him or giving him candy to eat. The person who goes to a concert when he is physically ill may find that his pain$_2$ prevents him from achieving his pleasure$_1$, and if he goes after just having broken up with his girl friend he may find that his pain$_1$ inhibits his pleasure$_1$. Sustained pain$_1$ may give rise to the pain$_2$ of psychosomatic diseases, and the sustained pleasure$_1$ of love may decidedly enhance the localized pleasures$_2$ of sexual intercourse. Possibilities for exploring causal connections between "higher" and "lower" pleasures and pains seem both interesting and endless.

To return now to Mill's question about the meaning of differences of quality in pleasure, we must insist that explicating the meaning of the psychological claim that pleasures differ qualitatively is not the same as accepting or rejecting the normative features of a qualitatively hedonistic answer to the question "What things are intrinsically good?" Before a philosophical position can be accepted or rejected, it must first be clearly understood. Pleasures (and pains) do seem to differ qualitatively as well as quantitatively, and the psychological thesis of qualitative hedonism at least makes sense. Critics of Mill's qualitative hedonism usually claim that in adopting it, Mill was really abandoning hedonism altogether in favor of some pluralistic or ideal utilitarian alternative, and we shall explore this criticism in detail in Chapter 5.

There is no doubt that certain features of traditional quantitative hedonism are abandoned by qualitative hedonism. For example, quantitative hedonists have usually assumed the linguistic thesis that where two or more things are called by a common name, a common property exists; but accepting qualitative hedonism is tantamount to rejecting this linguistic thesis. Also, the assumption that the relative value of intrinsically good states of conscious feeling can be determined by measuring merely the duration, intensity, and causal connections of these states is abandoned by qualitative hedonism in its insistence that other things being equal, a higher pleasure may be less intense or prolonged than a lower one and still be *better*. Qualitative hedonism calls for new and nonquantitative ways of measuring worth, and however successful or unsuccessful it was, Mill's "consensus of experienced judges" test was an attempt to provide such a way of measurement. This also will be further explored in Chapter 5.

The theory of qualitative hedonism to be developed in this book will include some of the following features, which will be more thoroughly and systematically discussed in Chapter 4. It will be maintained that instead of a single quality of pleasantness which all "pleasures" have in common, there are instead innumerable qualitatively different feelings that we like and wish to sustain and repeat. Furthermore, some of these qualitatively different feelings seem to be inseparable in practice and even in logic from their so-called "sources" or "objects," since they cannot be fully distinguished from or identified independently of some of the nonaffective properties of these objects. Not only are there two classes of agreeable feelings—localized and nonlocalized—but within each class there are qualitative and perhaps even valuational differences among the feelings. For example, we enjoy the localized pleasures of eating peppermint ice cream, drinking hot tea, soaking our feet in hot water, and having our backs rubbed. But even these localized enjoyments do not have a single quality of pleasantness in common. Instead, each of them has its own *distinctive* feeling tone which we like and wish to sustain and repeat. The same sort of thing must be said for localized pains. The pain of novocain as it wears off is qualitatively distinct from the pain of the needle that inserted it into the gum, and both of these are distinctly different from the pain of toothache or of a drill without novocain. Such oral pains are again quite distinct qualitatively from the pain of a bee sting, burn, abrasion, pin prick, or the breathlessness of emphysema. The distinctive feeling tone of many specific pains or pleasures cannot be fully identified in direct experience, thought, or imagination independently of some of the nonaffective properties of their "sources" or "objects." This is also true of examples of nonlocalized enjoyment and suffering. The intrinsically good nonlocalized feelings of rational contemplation and inquiry are available only in conjunction with rational contemplation and inquiry; those of love, friendship, and other forms of personal intimacy are derivable only from love, friendship, and other forms of personal intimacy. Similarly, the sufferings of guilt, loneliness, boredom, despair, and so on are not available to us in total separation from those emotions and beliefs which constitute grief, guilt, loneliness, alienation, boredom, and despair. There is no way for qualified judges to "isolate" any of these distinctive feelings totally from the nonaffective properties of their intentional objects, even in imagination, to determine if anything of intrinsic value or disvalue is lost or gained in the absence of these objects. The pleasures of contemplation (or of eating peppermint ice cream) would not be just those pleasures in the absence of contemplation (or of the taste of peppermint ice cream). Nor would the pain of grief or the pain of a toothache be just those pains in total isolation from the nonaffective properties that they accompany in experience, thought, and imagination. "Pleasure" and "pain" concepts are usually intentional concepts, just as are the concepts of "desire" and "consciousness."[20]

One way of understanding a theory is to explore the significant ways in which it differs from major competing theories. We now have a sufficient grasp of qualitative hedonism to enable us to examine its contrast with traditional quantitative hedonism, particularly with respect to their answers to the question "What things are intrinsically good?" We shall attempt to show that traditional quantitative hedonism is conceptually, psychologically, and ethically inadequate and to explain why qualitative hedonism is not committed to its embarrassing implications.

3

A Critique of Quantitative Hedonism

In maintaining that pleasure or happiness defined in terms of pleasure is the only intrinsic good, and that pain or unhappiness defined in terms of pain is the only intrinsic bad, the quantitative hedonist makes certain psychological and linguistic assumptions which are quite different from those of the qualitative hedonist. He presupposes the linguistic thesis that the word "pleasure" always refers to one and the same inner quality of feeling, as does the word "pain." He presupposes also the psychological thesis that the agreeable feeling that we get from one source is the same in quality, though not necessarily in intensity or duration, as the agreeable feeling that we get from any other source; and the same sort of thing is true of disagreeable feeling. "Pleasure is pleasure" and "pain is pain" no matter how we get them. If both these assumptions are false, as has been suggested in Chapter 2, then linguistic and psychological considerations provide perfectly adequate rational grounds for rejecting quantitative hedonism, even if no normative issues are raised. If quantitative hedonism rests on linguistic and psychological confusion, then it is not a viable normative alternative to qualitative hedonism or pluralism from the very outset.

Just for the sake of the argument, however, let us tentatively grant the quantitative hedonist his assumptions, and let us assume, as most traditional ethics texts do, that quantitative hedonism is an intelligible alternative normative answer to the question of what is intrinsically good and bad. There is still much more to be said about this theory than what is usually said about it. One way of examining a position philosophically is to see what it logically entails, and to ask ourselves if these logical implications are acceptable to us.

Most traditional discussions of hedonism call attention to one implication of the hedonistic claim that only pleasure or happiness is intrinsically good, namely that all so-called "pluralistic goods" are merely instrumental goods, of great importance perhaps as sources of agreeable feeling or as ways of avoiding disagreeable feeling, but of no intrinsic worth. Another important logical implication of quantitative hedonism never seems to get discussed, however. There is good reason to suspect that most self-professed quantitative hedonists have not been fully aware of the clear implication of their position, which we shall call "the replaceability thesis," that since all so-called pluralistic goods are merely of instrumental value, and since "pleasure is pleasure" no matter what its source, then each pluralistic good could in principle be replaced by an equally efficient or more efficient source of agreeable feeling without any loss of intrinsic worth. All instrumental goods are in principle expendable if other equally efficient sources of agreeable feeling, or ways of avoiding disagreeable feeling, can be provided. The pluralistic goods may be *standard* sources of happiness, given our way of organizing society; but there is nothing about any of them which makes them *necessary* conditions of human happiness.

There is a distinction to be made between particular and standard (nearly universal) sources of enjoyment. A particular source of happiness is a cause of happiness for limited groups of people who share limited interests, but a standard source of happiness is a cause of happiness for almost everyone, at least in a given cultural tradition. The hedonist should and usually does point out that being an effective hedonist requires a great deal of knowledge of both human nature in general and one's own individual nature. It is not enough to know what usually gives most men pleasure; we must also know ourselves and what sources of pleasure are especially effective in our own particular case. I, along with a limited group of other persons, may enjoy fishing; but you may not. You, along with a few others, may enjoy poetry; but I may not. For each of us, according to quantitative hedonism, it is only the enjoyment that is worthwhile for its own sake; and it is only the particular sources of enjoyment we utilize which vary.

Some sources of enjoyment are almost universal, however. These sources are generally efficient means to the end of producing agreeable feeling and preventing or eliminating disagreeable feeling, at least in most advanced Western cultures as we have known them, even if not for all human cultures. The "pluralistic goods" we shall mention shortly answer to this description. Most quantitative hedonists may have assumed that these things are necessary sources of happiness, but their position implies logically that these sources are just as expendable in principle as any of the more particular or idiosyncratic ones if another set of sources of happiness that works just as well or perhaps a little bit better can be provided in their place. Any of the pluralistic goods are only instrumental goods and as such are in principle and perhaps even in practice replaceable without loss of intrinsic worth.

Now, the pluralist can agree with the hedonist that his intrinsic goods are sources of agreeable feeling, and that they may be regarded as instrumental goods in that sense; but he wants to insist that this is not the whole story about them. In addition, he maintains, there is something intrinsically desirable or worthwhile about these things; they are not *merely* instrumental goods. It should be understood that the hedonist cannot win his case against the pluralist by showing that pluralistic goods are instrumental goods, though this is as far as his arguments usually take him. He must prove the stronger thesis that they are *merely* instrumental goods. Correspondingly, the pluralist must show that they are *more than* merely instrumental goods, while at the same time conceding that they are *at least* that.

Many candidates for the status of intrinsic good have been offered by philosophers and nonphilosophers. Without attempting to provide an exhaustive list of these, we can at least mention some of the more important and representative things which pluralists have presented as worth having, experiencing, preserving, and acquiring for their own sakes. No pluralist need be committed to everything we shall mention, for if there is *just one thing* other than pleasure which we regard as inherently good and worthwhile, then we are pluralists. We shall discuss such possible nonhedonistic intrinsic goods as freedom, interpersonal intimacy or love, beauty, art, creativity, knowledge and truth, and moral virtue and activity.

It is not easy to decide where we stand on the question of pluralism versus hedonism, especially when there are both quantitative and qualitative forms of the latter. But if we concentrate on quantitative hedonism for the moment, it is illuminating to ask ourselves whether we can accept all the logical implications of the position, especially the "replaceability thesis," according to which all pluralistic goods are in principle replaceable without loss of intrinsic worth by equally efficient sources of agreeable feeling. As we reflect on these pluralistic goods, we must ask ourselves throughout the discussion: Is there anything here for the loss of which we would not be fully compensated by being provided with an equally efficient source of agreeable feeling? If our answer is negative, then we probably are not quantitative hedonists.

Pluralistic Goods and Brave New World

Among its many virtues, Aldous Huxley's *Brave New World* (first published in 1932) has the great merit of showing us what it might be like to live in a social order in which most of the pluralistic goods that are standard for our society have been virtually eliminated, or at least severely limited or modified, and replaced by an even more efficient set of sources of agreeable feeling. Keep in mind that *Brave New World* only illustrates the *replaceability* of pluralistic goods considered merely as sources of happiness. It does not show that this replacement occurs without loss of intrinsic worth. Whether value is lost is a question we must decide for ourselves in the most enlightened way possible while drawing out the logical implications of quantitative hedonism.

Some imagination is required to envision a world such as Huxley describes, but his vision is not sheer fancy. It is closer to prophecy, for developments in technology, science, and society have made it, or soon will make it, a realistic open possibility for the future of our own world order, if we so choose. In fact, Huxley suggests that it may even be an inevitability in the next century, whether we so choose or not.[1]

Freedom in the sense of civil liberty has been regarded by many as an intrinsic good whose significance is not exhausted by the fact that it is enjoyable and tends to lead to more of the same. Formally, civil liberty consists in a politically or constitutionally guaranteed set of human rights to behave in certain specified ways without social or governmental hindrance, as for example those rights specified in the Bill of Rights to the Constitution of the United States. Materially, such freedom consists in the active exercise of these rights. It is freedom in this material sense, as involving activities permitted and protected by the rights of freedom of religion, speech, inquiry, thought, assembly, and so on, which is the viable candidate for the status of nonhedonistic good. In *Brave New World* virtually no one has such freedom, for the masses are told what to believe, how to behave, what to say, and when to assemble by a small group of experts who make all the decisions. Freedom is replaced by something approximating absolute social stability, the primary function of which is to remove pain and frustration. This is the negative half of the program that must be implemented in any hedonistic utopia, the other half being the providing of sources of positive agreeable feeling. Huxley's society does that quite effectively too, as we shall see; and without civil liberty the citizens of *Brave New World* have all their waking moments constantly flooded by agreeable feeling, with almost no disagreeable feeling at all. They are perfectly happy, but is anything of intrinsic worth sacrificed in the interest of happiness?

Interpersonal intimacy or love is a deep and enduring emotional involvement with and appreciation for the full concreteness and uniqueness of another being, normally a human being. It is the intrinsic evaluation of another person as an individual person, and it involves regarding and treating another person as an end himself and never merely as a means to some other end. Such involvement and appreciation do not always characterize interpersonal relations, but there are certain types of relationship, such as friendship, marriage, and various family connections, in which they typically develop when they appear at all. This kind of involvement is usually part of an ideal expectation of marriage and the family. In friendship, it seems to arise out of common interests and a common world view. In marriage, the element of sex is added, and in other family relations a common heritage replaces sex as the initial tie that binds persons, in ideal instances, into relationships of interpersonal intimacy. Although quantitative hedonists have generally assumed that some such relationships are essential sources of human happiness, they must eventually face up to the fact that they are at best merely standard sources, given our traditional Western ways of ordering society. In principle they too are expendable, and *Brave New World* presents us with an alternative way of ordering society in which they are dispensed with in practice. Friendship, marriage, and family are all taboo in this new world order, being replaced by constant but superficial interpersonal contacts that are never allowed to develop into anything deep, enduring, or unique; depth of attachment is prevented by the simple expedient of making it impossible for any two persons to spend a great deal of time together. Completely free sex replaces marriage, and the pleasures of going to bed with a different sexual partner every night would presumably be more than adequate compensation, on purely quantitatively hedonistic grounds, for any loss of marital intimacy or love.

Beauty and art have been regarded by many pluralists as intrinsic goods, as well as sources of enjoyment. Beauty is not completely eliminated in *Brave New World,* but by a process of extensive conditioning most of the citizens are desensitized to the beauty of nature, and since the fine arts do not exist, people have no opportunity to enjoy their beauty or their challenge. Flowers, trees, skies, sunsets are still there in this new social order, but the state has made it impossible for its citizens to appreciate their beauty, mainly because natural beauty is too cheap and makes no significant contribution to economic stability. In the interest of job security, its citizens are conditioned to be consumers of mass-produced artifacts. Art, in the sense of the advanced "fine arts" of painting, music, sculpture, poetry, literature, and drama, is virtually eliminated as being too much of a threat to social stability and uniformity and the happiness which these in turn make possible. As the World Controller explains:

> "But that's the price we have to pay for stability. You've got to choose between happiness and what people used to call high art. We've sacrificed the high art. We have the feelies and the scent organ instead."
>
> "But they don't mean anything."
>
> "They mean themselves; they mean a lot of agreeable sensations to the audience."[2]

Our movies, which stimulate only the senses of hearing and sight, are dreadfully inefficient sources of agreeable feeling by comparison with the feelies, which stimulate the tactile senses and taste and smell in addition to sight and hearing. Constant access to them is provided, and whenever citizens feel a need for another shot of happiness (sustained agreeable feeling) they can go and get it. And they may get any intensity of it they desire by turning the appropriate knobs. If it is complained that the feelies are poor substitutes for the fine arts since the latter provide nonlocalized agreeable feeling, we must remember that the quantitative hedonist cannot regard this distinction, even if he acknowledges it, as involving a difference in quality. Pleasure is pleasure, no matter what its source. Since intensity of pleasure depends merely on turning a knob, an hour at the feelies is surely worth at least as much as and probably more than an hour at the art museum in purely quantitative terms. Remember Bentham's dictum: "Prejudice apart, the game of push-pin is of equal value with the arts and sciences of music and poetry." Or is it?

Knowledge and truth have been presented by many pluralists as intrinsic goods. Granted that some things are too trivial to know, and some things are worth knowing only as means to other ends, nevertheless there are things worth knowing for their own sake, even if we are pained by that knowledge, pluralists have held. That God exists, that other human minds exist, or that we are loved by another person who is not merely faking it, even some items of scientific truth, have been thought to be truths valuable in and of themselves. Now quantitative hedonists have maintained from the time of Epicurus that knowledge and truth are only instrumental goods, useful both in avoiding pain and as positive sources of enjoyment. It would be inaccurate to suggest that the citizens of *Brave New World* have learned how to dispense with knowledge altogether, for this is a civilization based upon a great deal of knowledge of applied science, engineering, and technology. However, those forms of knowledge that pluralists regard as intrinsically good, both in their pursuit and in their possession, are conspicuously absent. History is bunk, and the greatest pains are taken to insure that the citizens have no access to the world's great literature, novels, poetry, drama, and essays. They are completely deprived of the opportunity to study comparative religion and the world's great religious scriptures and writings. They know no philosophy, being exposed to only one possible world-view, the official but simple doctrine of their social order. They have no ability for critical thinking in the areas of metaphysical, ethical, religious, or political belief. And the gnawing, unpleasant uncertainty of unfixated belief, generated by acquaintance with multiple possibilities, does not trouble them. Even pure science is forbidden as too dangerous to stability and happiness, only "cookbook science" being permitted. A hedonistic utopia based upon an already developed technology has no need for further pure knowledge or for the liberal arts and humanities. Happiness can be assured without them. Vocational training and cookbook science suffice for the purely quantitative pursuit of happiness.

Moral virtue and activity have been offered frequently as intrinsically worthwhile goods, but even here the quantitative

57

hedonist is committed to the possibility of their being replaced by other equally efficient sources of happiness. *Brave New World* shows how it might actually be done. The basic problem of instilling a code of conduct designed to harmonize conflicting interests and promote the general welfare is solved by intensive social conditioning. Motivation to be moral, to act on the society's rules (which are not *our* rules, of course) is provided by conditioning, well-developed social reinforcement, and, last but not least, by the drug *soma,* which makes it possible for the citizens to carry half of their morality around with them in a bottle. No painful effort to be virtuous is ever required. As the World Controller explains the matter:

> My dear young friend, civilization has absolutely no need of nobility or heroism. These things are symptoms of political inefficiency. In a properly organized society like ours, nobody has any opportunities for being noble or heroic. Conditions have got to be thoroughly unstable before the occasion can arise. Where there are wars, where there are divided alliances, where there are temptations to be resisted, objects of love to be fought for or defended—there, obviously, nobility and heroism have some sense. But there aren't any wars nowadays. The greatest care is taken to prevent you from loving any one too much. There's no such thing as a divided allegiance; you're so conditioned that you can't help doing what you ought to do. And what you ought to do is on the whole so pleasant, so many of the natural impulses are allowed free play, that there really aren't any temptations to resist. And if ever, by some unlucky chance, anything unpleasant should somehow happen, why, there's always *soma* to give you a holiday from the facts. And there's always *soma* to calm your anger, to reconcile you to your enemies, to make you patient and long-suffering. In the past you could only accomplish these things by making a great effort and after years of hard moral training. Now, you swallow two or three half-gramme tablets, and there you are. Anybody can be virtuous now. You can carry at least half your morality about in a bottle. Christianity without tears—that's what *soma* is.[3]

Although the Brave New Worlders have a moral code and adequate motivation to abide by it, being moral for them never involves effortful moral activity and self-development. Would the availability of such a wonder drug as *soma* adequately compensate us for their loss? The World Controller, who conceived of happiness in purely quantitative terms, insists that "happiness is never grand."[4]

As Huxley envisioned it, *soma* is the perfect drug. It relieves pain and anxiety, and it induces euphoria as well. Properly used, it has no harmful aftereffects; it results in rehabilitation and refreshment rather than depletion and debility. Properly used, it is the perfect source of happiness, and unlike most of our drugs it never leads to a preponderance of pain over pleasure in the long run. It is such an effective euphorogenic agent that it could effectively replace *any* of our standard pluralistic goods as a means to happiness, quantitatively conceived. It is a catchall substitute for everything, having "all the advantages of Christianity and alcohol; none of their defects."[5] "And if anything should go wrong, there's *soma*."[6] Would the availability of such a drug really compensate us for the loss of any pluralistic good that might be offered? With such a drug, quantity of pleasure would be not merely equal but superior; and *soma* would be at least as good as poetry, music, philosophy, or any other source of agreeable feeling that might be mentioned. But are such quantitative considerations alone relevant to the determination of what has intrinsic worth? If our answer is negative, then it is doubtful that we are quantitative hedonists.

Quantitative hedonism entails the thesis that if all pluralistic goods are merely of instrumental worth, and pleasure is pleasure no matter how we get it, then all pluralistic goods are *in principle* replaceable without loss of intrinsic worth by equally efficient sources of sustained agreeable feeling or happiness. *Brave New World* illustrates how it might be possible in practice so to order society that these goods are replaced by another

59

extremely efficient set of sources of sustained agreeable feeling. We must decide for ourselves in the most enlightened way possible whether this replacement could occur without loss of anything of intrinsic worth.

Can Electrodes Make Us Happy?

If the pluralists' standard goods are replaceable when considered merely as instrumental goods, we should fully understand that all the sources of pleasure in *Brave New World* such as free sex, the feelies, and *soma* are also expendable. Just as none of our standard sources of enjoyment are really needed, so none of the sources which are standard in *Brave New World* are essential either. If the ideal is sustained agreeable feeling during all our wakeful moments with no disagreeable feeling intermixed, we now know that this state is attainable by merely hooking up a set of well-placed electrodes to the "pleasure centers" of the brain and stimulating the brain with mild electric shocks. Male rats that have been taught to turn on the electricity by pushing a lever seem to prefer this source of happiness to any now standard sources of ratty pleasures. They will press the lever to the point of physical collapse in preference to eating and drinking, and even in preference to copulating with an available female rat in heat. In both animal and human subjects, implanted electrodes have already been left in place for a number of years without objectionable consequences. Suppose that we knew how to sustain life and awareness for years and years with little or no physical exercise. If we had a chance, under those conditions, to consign ourselves to a hospital bed attached to a well-placed set of electrodes for the next fifty or sixty years of our life, but with no other type of human activity, experience, or fulfillment, would we take it? This particular way of getting sustained agreeable feeling seems to be as efficient as anything imaginable, and obviously more efficient than our pluralist's standard goods as a source of sheer quantity of constant agreeable feeling with no disagreeable feeling intermixed. If contrast is required for recognition, we could be allowed to turn on and off the electricity as often as we liked, and the quantity of electricity fed into the electrodes could be varied, giving highs and lows of pleasure, but no pain. Furthermore, there is nothing inherently egoistic about wanting to be so stimulated. Granted, a few people would be needed to supply and maintain the hospitals. We could teach them to be happy in their ability to make so many other people happy. The quantitatively hedonistic moral ideal of the greatest happiness for the greatest number of people would seem to be well satisfied by having the largest possible number of people hooked up to such electrodes for the largest possible portion of life. Although there may be insurmountable practical obstacles to the universal implementation of such an ideal, nevertheless we should be able to accept in principle the clear implication of quantitative hedonism that electrodes can make us supremely happy. If we cannot accept this implication of the replaceability thesis at least in principle, then again it is very doubtful that we are quantitative hedonists.

The quantitative hedonist might still resist choosing to be the sort of full-time electrode operator we have just envisioned on the practical grounds that lack of physical exercise will result in physical degeneracy and greatly shorten life and with it the enjoyment which being alive makes possible. However, it seems that he could not reject on his own purely quantitative grounds the opportunity to become the sort of part-time electrode operator envisioned by J. J. C. Smart in the following passage, for such a mode of life is already feasible given even the present state of medical technology. As we shall see, something very much like it has already been made available to a number of human subjects. Smart paints the verbal picture of

the voluptuary of the future, a bald-headed man with a number of electrodes protruding from his skull, one to give the physical pleasure of sex, one for that of eating, one for that of drinking, and so on. Now is this the sort of life that all our ethical planning should culminate in? A few hours' work a week, automatic factories, comfort and security from disease, and hours spent at a switch, continually electrifying various regions of one's brain? Surely not. Men were made for higher things, one can't help wanting to say, even though one knows that men weren't made for anything, but are the product of evolution by natural selection.[7]

There are difficulties with the part-time electrode operator, however, which at first seem to make our argument very inconclusive. The basic difficulty is that there might be some explanation other than our not being quantitative hedonists for our unwillingness to concede that the life of the leisure-time electrode devotee is the best possible form of human existence, or at least that it is as good as any. Smart suggests that our unwillingness to accept such an application of quantitative hedonism might be due to confusion rather than to clarity. It might, he maintains, involve a confusion of our appraisal of "the possibility of (a) our being contented if we are in a certain state, and (b) our being contented at the prospect of being so contented."[8] As he explains the relevance of this distinction to our electrode example:

> Perhaps a possible reluctance to call the electrode operator "happy" might come from the following circumstance. The electrode operator might be perfectly contented, might perfectly enjoy his electrode operating, and might not be willing to exchange his lot for any other. And we ourselves, perhaps, once we became electrode operators too, could become perfectly contented and satisfied. We want other things, perhaps to write a book or get into a cricket team. If someone said "from tomorrow onwards you are going to be forced to be an electrode operator" we should not be pleased. Maybe from tomorrow onwards, once the electrode work had started, we should be perfectly contented, but we are not contented now at the prospect. We are not satis-

fied at being told that we would be in a certain state from tomorrow onwards, even though we may know that from tomorrow
onwards we should be perfectly satisfied. All this is psychologically possible.[9]

Now the real philosophical issue here is not whether it is
psychologically possible for us to confuse the situation of the
experiencer of electrode-induced happiness with that of an
external observer who does not wish to be such an experiencer.
No doubt our aversion to such happiness might involve just
such confusion, but on the other hand it is certainly quite possible that it might involve no confusion whatsoever. The relevant philosophical issue is whether it is reasonable for us to
have such an aversion, whether there are any grounds for it
which would justify our unwillingness to be a happy electrode
addict. There can be little doubt that on the grounds of purely
quantitative considerations, we can have no good reason for
aversion. In sheer quantity of agreeable feeling free from discomfort, the life made available to us by electrodes would be at
least equal to and probably superior to any other form of life.
If we are quantitative hedonists, there are no grounds for our
preferring to write books or play cricket; and our aversion to
electrode happiness is quite irrational. We may have ground-
less, irrational aversions, to be sure, but philosophical positions
cannot be defended by appealing to them.

On the other hand, if we are not quantitative hedonists,
there might be perfectly clear-headed reasons for our aversion
to electrode-induced happiness, involving no confusion whatsoever between present aversion and future contentment. The
qualitative hedonist might resist electrode-induced happiness
because he thinks that certain *qualities* of pleasure would be
absent in electrode euphoria and is not content with sheer
quantity of a limited spectrum of kinds of pleasure, however
prolonged and intense. Part of Smart's explanation for our

unwillingness to call the electrode operator "happy" is that we do consider more than contentment (absence of pain) and frequency of enjoyment when we apply this word. In addition to including such quantitative considerations, he holds, we use the word "in part to express a favourable attitude to the idea of such a form of contentment and enjoyment."[10] Now this is perfectly true, but the acknowledgment that there are *different forms* of contentment or enjoyment is itself a tacit abandonment of quantitative hedonism. Of course, this could merely mean that there are different *sources* of contentment or enjoyment, but then we have to concede that it is irrational for the quantitative hedonist to prefer one source to another when they are both equally efficient in producing intensity and duration of pleasure. If, however, we mean that our contentments and enjoyments *themselves* vary in form or quality, and that we rate some of these qualitatively distinct enjoyments so highly that we are not willing to apply the word "happy" where they are missing, then we are qualitative hedonists and are rejecting the happiness of the electrode operator on qualitatively hedonistic grounds.

The preceding argument assumes, however, that we know at least indirectly what kinds of pleasures would and would not be experienced by electrode operators, and also that we know that there are some kinds or qualities of pleasure which are not duplicated by electronic stimulation. If we allow analogical reasoning about other minds, we can know both the kinds of pleasures that would and those that would not be experienced by rats or pigs when the pleasure centers of their brains are electronically stimulated. It is stimulation of the septal region, the sexual centers of the brain, which yields the results indicating that laboratory animals prefer such stimulation to food or females in heat, even at the price of a bit of pain. Now, in recent years, human brains have been extensively subjected to such electrode stimulation, and stimulation of the septal region in human subjects yields primarily localized sexual pleasures and sexual fantasies. Presumably, the septally stimulated rat is getting some modified mousey analogue of localized sexual pleasure and sexual fantasy of sufficient intensity and duration to prompt it to prefer this source to the relatively transient enjoyments of a female in heat, of food, of drink, and so on. We can also know that there are certain valuable *kinds* of pleasures that rats, pigs, and other animals cannot enjoy, however valuable sexual pleasure may be in its own right. No organism is capable of experiencing qualities of pleasure derivable only from capacities which it lacks, even from electronic stimulation. No amount of electronic stimulation will make a rat or a pig experience the philosophical pleasures of a Socrates rationally examining life, or the creative raptures of a Newton formulating for the first time the laws of gravity, or the paternal or maternal joys of a human parent nurturing a distinctively human child to maturity. Many qualities of enjoyment available to beings with human capacities are simply not available by any means to rats or pigs, no matter how well satisfied they may be with their own forms of enjoyment. Humans thus have a perfectly rational qualitatively hedonistic justification for preferring a distinctively human mode of experience, for a much greater variety of qualities of pleasure is available to human subjects. But although we have a good reason for not wanting to be well-satisfied electronically stimulated rats or pigs, the question still remains whether the same justification provides us with a good reason for not wanting to be well-satisfied electronically stimulated human beings.

In recent years, a number of human subjects whose brains are being electronically stimulated have been extensively studied by Dr. Robert G. Heath and his associates at Tulane University School of Medicine. The doctors' findings, reported in a number of articles,[11] indicate that while some pleasures of a nonsexual nature have been produced through stimulation of other parts of the brain, this technique has not been a great success in generating nonsexual pleasures. By far the most intense and prolonged pleasures have resulted consistently from stimulation of the septal region. As reported to the researchers by their experimental human subjects, the pleasures thus produced are primarily sexual pleasures involving sexual desire, sexual fantasy, preorgasmic enjoyment, and occasionally orgasm itself. The most rewarding pleasure centers of the brain thus seem to be its sexual centers. Not only may extremely intense and continuous euphoria be thus induced over a period of several hours at a time, given present technology, but such stimulation of the septum also immediately terminates all pre-existent painful emotions and feelings. Some frustration over the inability to reach orgasm may occasionally result. Nevertheless, septal stimulation is most consistently preferred by subjects allowed to choose from a variety of buttons activating electrodes in various parts of their own brains. Pain centers of the brain have also been identified, but subjects do not elect to stimulate them.

Now, a purely quantitative hedonist should be content with the intense and prolonged sexual pleasures that even present medical technology could make available to him during his leisure time by electronic brain stimulation. Such "happiness" would be at least as intense and prolonged as that derivable from any other source. Why spend one's leisure hours reading Plato or even risking the pains one might receive from a real live sexual partner when electrodes can thus make us happy in a purely quantitative sense of happiness? The quantitative hedonist maintains pleasure is pleasure no matter how we get it and that it is reasonable to prefer one pleasure as such to another only on grounds of greater intensity or duration. We might, of course, reject the life of the leisure-time electrode operator on the grounds that although the quantity of pleasure thus obtained is as great as in any available form of life, never-

66

theless the qualitative variety of pleasure thus obtainable is far too limited; but then we would be qualitative and not quantitative hedonists.

Though we are at present infinitely far removed from being able to do this, let us consider what would be logically implied if it were possible for us to duplicate by electronic stimulation at least the leisure-time equivalent of all the qualities of experience and feeling available to us in the richest imaginable *qualitatively* hedonistic paradise in all their variety, intensity, duration, and concreteness. Such a world might include the enjoyment of incredible philosophical creativity and contemplation, all the concrete positive adventures of a happy marriage and family life, all the Bach cantatas and Beethoven symphonies one can absorb, and all the similar pleasures imaginable. Given the prospect of uninterrupted enjoyment of such an electronically simulated universe at least during our leisure time, and the assurance that no one in the "real" world would ever be hurt by our enjoyment of it, might we not be logically constrained to choose the life of the human electrode operator on qualitatively hedonistic grounds? In principle, yes; but in practice, no. We are infinitely far removed from being able to create such a qualitatively hedonistic paradise electronically, though we are already able to produce a quantitatively hedonistic paradise by such means. As idealist philosophers have always insisted, the concrete world of everyday experience would be no less reliable or interesting if caused by God than by matter, as common sense assumes. The same would be true of a qualitatively rich universe of enjoyable experience produced by electronic stimulation; and "prejudice apart," as Bentham might say, there would be no grounds *in principle* for not choosing such a universe. Even the pluralist would have to choose it if it contained all his pluralistic goods. In practice, however, the electrodes simply cannot do what God can do; and there we shall probably always have to leave it.

Quantitative and Qualitative Senses of "More Pleasant"

Let us forget about fictional Brave New Worlds and electronically simulated universes of experience for a moment and return to realistic prospects for happiness in our more familiar world. It seems entirely possible that a quantitative hedonist might maintain that neither of the fictional but possible worlds of happiness we have examined would be nearly as desirable as the best available edition of our day-to-day world. A universe of experience containing all the standard pluralistic goods as sources of happiness might still be greatly to be preferred to that of *Brave New World* or the electrode operator simply because at its best it would contain *more pleasure* than either. The strongest possible form of quantitative hedonism might be one which claims that at its best ordinary life involving social intercourse, moral effort and activity, aesthetic experience, and a sense of personal identity and integrity is simply the *most pleasant* world imaginable, containing within it the greatest possible duration and intensity of agreeable feeling.

Now it is true that a reasonable person might greatly prefer ordinary life at its best to the hedonic utopias we have examined, but it is not at all clear that he would do so on purely quantitative grounds. It probably is true in some sense that our ordinary world at its best would be "more pleasant" than our hedonic utopias, and doubtless we may be misled into thinking that we are indeed quantitative hedonists because we prefer this more pleasant prospect. The difficulty is that there are both quantitative and qualitative senses of "more pleasant," that we do not properly recognize this, and that we may be deceived by the seemingly quantitative word "more" into thinking that our preferences are based on the purely quantitative considerations to which the quantitative hedonist calls our attention.

68

What does the quantitative hedonist mean by "more pleas-ant?" He means (a) that there is one and only one quality of agreeable feeling that we call "pleasure" which is exemplified in all pleasant experiences; (b) that this one quality of pleasure may be exemplified in different experiences for different lengths of time or duration and in different degrees of inten-sity; (c) that any two pleasures as such may be compared only in such quantitative ways as intensity and duration; and (d) that the "more pleasant" experience is either the one which lasts the longer or the more intense, or some combination of the two. If he holds that our ordinary world at its best is "more pleas-ant" than that of *Brave New World* or the leisure-time electrode operator, this must mean that these universes of experience all exemplify one and only one quality of agreeable feeling which we call "pleasure"; but this claim is false because there are *many* qualities of agreeable feeling which we call "pleasure." He must further mean merely that there is a greater intensity and dura-tion of this *one* feeling in our ordinary world at its best, which is also false because the difference between the ordinary world and the others is that there is a greater *variety* of qualities of pleasure in it, not a greater intensity and duration of one qual-ity of pleasure in it. The basic confusion involved is a confusion of "more variety" with "more degree and duration." Our ordi-nary world is simply not a quantitatively hedonistic world.

The qualitative hedonist is also entitled to say that our ordi-nary world at its best is "more pleasant" than that of our hedonistic utopias, but he means something quite different by the expression. He does not abandon quantitative considera-tions of intensity and duration, but he adds to these the follow-ing. "More pleasant" also means (a) containing a *greater variety* of those agreeable qualities of feeling which we call "plea-sures." Once qualitative variety is acknowledged, quantitative hedonism is abandoned once and for all. Now there is a sense

69

in which varieties of pleasure may be counted, just as varieties of color and odor may be counted, but in counting varieties we are not merely counting degrees and durations. "More pleasant" also means (b) that when two distinct qualities of agreeable feeling are compared, we prefer one to the other. Such qualitative preference is entirely independent of quantity of duration and intensity and is the sort of thing involved when Mill insisted that no quantity of "a beast's pleasures" should be preferred over the distinctively human pleasures of the life of the mind or the sense of human dignity. Qualitatively distinct pleasures may be preferentially ranked on grounds of *qualitative* superiority or inferiority, and their ranking need not vary directly with changes in duration and intensity. Such a ranking yields another sense of "more pleasant" not available to the quantitative hedonist. It is perhaps best characterized as an ordinal rather than as a cardinal meaning of "more pleasant." We may rank pleasures as first, second, third, and so on in order of qualitative superiority and inferiority and are not at all limited to cardinal countings of durations and intensities.

Cardinal comparisons of intensities and durations properly take place when we are comparing two instances of *the same quality* of pleasure. We may say, for example, that today's experience of localized sexual pleasure lasted for three minutes and yesterday's for thirty minutes and that the intensity of the former registered five on our subjective hedometer whereas the latter registered only three. Cardinal comparisons of intensity and duration have no use, however, when we are dealing with two entirely distinct qualities of pleasure, and we must resort to ordinal rankings. We must not confuse the intensity of our rational preference for an agreeable feeling with the intensity of the preferred feeling itself. This position was made quite clear by Francis Hutcheson, whose interpretation of qualitative hedonism probably had a great influence on John Stuart Mill. Hutcheson wrote:

As to pleasures of the same kind, 'tis manifest their values are in joint proportion of their intenseness and duration. In estimating the duration, we not only regard the constancy of the object, or its remaining in our power, and the duration of the sensations it affords, but the constancy of our fancy or relish: for when this changes it puts an end to the enjoyment.

In comparing pleasures of different kinds, the value is as the duration and dignity of the kind jointly. We have an immediate sense of a dignity, a perfection, or beatifick quality in some kinds, which no intenseness of the lower kinds can equal, were they also as lasting as we could wish. No intenseness or duration of any external sensation gives it a dignity or worth equal to that of the improvement of the soul by knowledge, or the ingenious arts; and much less is it equal to that of virtuous affections and actions. We never hesitate in judging thus about the happiness or perfection of others, where the impetuous cravings of appetites and passions do not corrupt our judgments, as they do often in our case. By this intimate feeling of dignity, enjoyments and exercises of some kinds, tho' not of the highest degree of those kinds, are incomparably more excellent and beatifick than the most intense and lasting enjoyments of the lower kinds. Nor is duration of such importance to some higher kinds, as it is to the lower. The exercise of virtue for a short period, provided it be not succeeded by something vicious, is of incomparably greater value than the most lasting sensual pleasures.[12]

Hutcheson recognized the possibility of using seemingly quantitative words to express qualitative differences when he continued:

Now if we denote by intenseness, in a more general meaning, the degree in which any perceptions or enjoyments are beatifick, then their comparative values are in a compound proportion of their intenseness and duration. But to retain always in view the grand differences of the kinds, and to prevent any imaginations, that the intenser sensations of the lower kinds with sufficient duration may compleat our happiness; it may be more convenient to estimate enjoyments by their dignity and duration: dignity denoting the excellence of the kind, when those of different kinds are compared; and the intenseness of the sensations, when we compare those of the same kind.[13]

In conclusion, we may prefer our ordinary world at its best to that of our hedonic utopias because we regard the former as the "more pleasant" world. But it would be a terrible confusion to think that this preference is based merely on quantitative considerations of intensity and duration of a single quality of agreeable feeling common to all such worlds. Rather it is based on the recognition of a greater *variety* of qualities of agreeable feeling in our ordinary world at its best. It may also involve the judgments that some of these varieties have a worth or dignity which makes their value cardinally incommensurable with others, though they may be ordinally superior to others in intrinsic worth. For their loss there would be no adequate compensation.

4

A Systematic Exposition of Qualitative Hedonism

Unlike the quantitative hedonist, the qualitative hedonist advances the linguistic thesis that (1) the word "pleasure" refers to *many different* inner qualities of feeling which we find interesting and desire to sustain, cultivate, and repeat; and the word "pain" refers to many different inner qualities of feeling which we find objectionable and desire to terminate and avoid. The qualitative hedonist also advances the psychological thesis that (2) the agreeable feeling we get from one source need not be the same *in quality,* or in intensity or duration, as the agreeable feeling we get from another source; and the disagreeable feeling we get from one source need not be the same in quality, or in intensity or duration, as that we get from another source. There is the further normative thesis, based upon (1) and (2), that (3) some of the diverse feelings we call "pleasures" are intrinsically better than and ought to be chosen in preference to other such feelings, even where duration or intensity are equal or even less; and some of the diverse feelings we call

73

"pains" are intrinsically worse than and ought to be rejected in preference to other such feelings, even where duration or intensity are equal or even greater. From the foregoing assumptions, it follows (4) that if a source of intrinsically different and superior pleasure is replaced by an efficient source of quantitatively equal but intrinsically different and inferior pleasure, something of intrinsic worth *is* lost by the replacement. Quantity of pleasure being equal, pushpin is *not* as good as music or poetry. Later in the chapter, we shall argue that (5) in their generic sense, "pleasure" connotes "all those qualities of feeling that we like and normally desire to sustain and cultivate," and "pain" connotes "all those qualities of feeling that we dislike and normally desire to eliminate and avoid." Finally, it will be explained that (6) different species of pleasure and pain may be distinguished from one another either by their causes or effects, or by their intentional objects. The latter type of intentional pleasures and pains are logically bound to and inseparable from those additional properties of experience or predicates of thought which distinguish concrete instances of pleasure from one another and concrete instances of pain from one another.

With the foregoing theses in mind, let us now work out some of the details of an application and defense of qualitative hedonism. First of all, we shall review the "pluralistic goods" examined in the preceding chapter and suggest how qualitative hedonism might deal with the question of their intrinsic worth. Then we shall examine some historical anticipations of qualitative hedonism. Finally we shall explore the relations between desires and pleasures and pains. In Chapter 5 we shall deal with some still unanswered questions about the theory, such as: Is qualitative hedonism really a disguised form of pluralism? How can we tell which pleasures are intrinsically better, and which pains intrinsically worse, than others? What is the qualitatively hedonistic conception of happiness and the good life?

And finally, can a theory of action and obligation be derived from qualitative hedonism?

Qualitative Hedonism and Various Pluralistic Goods

There is a sense in which all the pluralistic goods discussed in Chapter 3 are instrumental goods and another sense in which they are intrinsic goods, though neither of these theses involves an abandonment of the central thesis of hedonism that intrinsic goodness is always located in agreeable feeling. All of the pluralistic goods may be used as means to *future* happiness, and in that use they must be considered as instrumental goods. At the same time, however, the *present* actualization of these pluralistic goods in human experience and activity is itself inherently enjoyable, even though it may have its price. The enjoyment here does not lie in the future but occurs simultaneously with and as an integral feature of the exercise and actualization of freedom; interpersonal intimacy or love; beauty, art, and creativity; knowledge, truth; moral virtue and activity, and other such goods not explicitly discussed in Chapter 3. Aristotle maintained that pleasure normally accompanies virtuous activities, and completes them as an end.[1] Aristotle understood the notions of both "activity" and "virtue" very broadly. By "activity" he meant the actualization of a real human potentiality. He included both sensing and contemplating as activities, rather than as passivities, as we today sometimes think of sensing. A "virtue" was any state of mind or activity which deserved praise for its own sake.

The exercise or actualization of freedom of speech and thought, regarded as sustained active processes, is normally accompanied by distinctive qualities of agreeable feeling, just as are the activities through which freedom of religion, the press, and assembly are actualized. If the disagreeable feelings of conflict and indecision are also generated, the actualization of freedom is still worth the price, especially when the horrible frustrations of coercion and tyranny are thrown into the calculus. The free exercise of thought is closely related to both the pursuit of knowledge and truth and the active contemplation of them when they have been caught. Both the pursuit of knowledge, the active process of satisfying our curiosity, and the contemplation of true belief supported by adequate evidence are inherently enjoyable activities—they involve exciting, interesting feelings that we wish to sustain and repeat, feelings quite different in quality from the interesting feelings of sexual orgasm or a back rub. Aristotle maintained that the pursuit and contemplation of metaphysical knowledge were utterly useless, but that such knowledge was nevertheless the very best kind. By this he meant to suggest that metaphysical truths will be true no matter what happens, so they do not enter directly into controlling events in such a way that one kind of thing will happen rather than another. He would not have understood his denial of the utility of metaphysics as entailing a denial of the view that the pursuit and contemplation of such knowledge are inherently enjoyable, however. He knew that the process of satisfying our metaphysical curiosity or of contemplating the results of such inquiry could be a means to the end of the enjoyment that accompanied the activity, and that in that sense metaphysical knowledge *was* useful. Aristotle wrote that "the activity of philosophic wisdom is admittedly the pleasantest of virtuous activities."[2] We must add that the active pursuit of and contemplation of knowledge in all the humanities, social sciences, and natural sciences as we know them are also inherently satisfying and enjoyable. The same sort of thing must be said of the concrete actualization of creative thinking in these areas of human knowledge, as well as of creativity in the fine arts such as literature, poetry, painting, music, and drama. The joys of creativity may be accompanied by the travails of mental birth, but they are different in kind from the joys of the feelies and the scent organ, and we cannot simply replace them by such joys without loss of intrinsic worth. Interpersonal intimacy or love as actualized in human experience and active interpersonal interaction with friends, mates, and loved ones is inherently enjoyable and not an easily replaceable means to an end that lies beyond itself. The appreciation of beauty in nature and the fine arts is also inherently pleasant, though the nonlocalized forms of pleasure derivable from such sources are not the same in quality or intrinsic worth as the localized forms of pleasure derived from eating sugar or soaking one's feet in hot water. Finally, effortful moral activity and self-development are themselves inherently enjoyable; and it is in this sense that the "virtue is its own reward" and that "the virtuous man is the happy man."

Let us pay just a bit more attention to this final point, since qualitative hedonism is able to make much sense of claims, often advanced, but not often justified, concerning the inherent and superior happiness of the virtuous man—the man who through effortful activity develops his own moral character to the point where acting virtuously is "second nature" to him, and who enjoys moral activity both before and after he has developed for himself the fixed, settled disposition to act in accord with virtue. Unlike Kant's man of virtue, Aristotle's good man did not continuously wrestle with painful temptation. Aristotle defined "happiness" as "activity of soul in accord with virtue," and though his definition makes no mention of pleasure, he elsewhere characterizes this virtuous activity which constitutes happiness as inherently pleasant:

> The man who does not rejoice in noble actions is not even good; since no one would call a man just who did not enjoy acting justly, nor any man liberal who did not enjoy liberal actions; and similarly in all other cases. If this is so, virtuous actions must be in themselves pleasant. But they are also *good* and *noble*, and have each of these attributes in the highest degree, since the good man

77

judges well about these attributes; his judgment is such as we
have described. Happiness then is the best, noblest, and most
pleasant thing in the world.[3]

We must not lose sight of the fact that living a virtuous life
often involves excruciatingly painful struggle against temptation. The pleasures of virtue must frequently be purchased
with the pain of moral struggle, and there are doubtless occa-
sions when virtue is not enjoyable, or at least not predomi-
nantly enjoyable. It would be foolhardy to maintain that virtue
is always fully its own reward in qualitatively hedonistic terms.
Yet it may be said that, at least under certain conditions, virtue
is its own reward in the sense that it is normally accompanied
by distinctive qualities of nonlocalized agreeable feeling which
are different from, superior to, and not replaceable by
localized agreeable feelings without loss of intrinsic worth. This
is true of many virtuous dispositions and activities that Aristotle
might not have been recognized as such, including forgiveness,
benevolence, loyalty, faith, hope, and love, as well as of many
dispositions and activities that Aristotle did discuss, such as
courage, wisdom, temperance, and justice. If our virtuous activities are expressions of and follow from a stable character, as
Aristotle required, then we will have that integrity which is the
essential condition for the enjoyment of virtue, conflicts of
interest will be minimized, and normal functioning will be accompanied by profound feelings of satisfaction. On the other
hand, if we have an unstable character, virtuous behavior may
be accompanied by painful feelings of conflict, doubt, irrita-
tion, and temptation.

If virtue is its own reward, at least at times, does it follow that
vice is its own punishment? It does not follow necessarily, but
there is also something to be said for this proposition. To claim
that all wicked activity is purely and inherently painful would
be too far-fetched. Malice, for example, by definition involves

taking pleasure in the thought of another's suffering. But at least some morally objectionable motives, dispositions, and kinds of actions are inherently painful in the sense that they involve as an integral part of themselves certain kinds of feelings which we dislike and normally wish to eliminate and avoid rather than sustain and cultivate. Hatred and anger, for example, involve inherently disagreeable feelings, and there is a very real sense in which a person who hates another or is angry with another may punish or make himself suffer more than he does the other. The pains here are qualitatively unlike the localized pains of a pin prick or a bee sting, and most of us find them to be intrinsically worse to live with as well. Bishop Butler, who probably did not recognize qualitative differences in pleasures and pains, seems nevertheless to have been correct in writing:

> Let it not be taken for granted that the temper of envy, rage, resentment, yields greater delight than meekness, forgiveness, compassion, and good-will; especially when it is acknowledged that rage, envy, resentment, are in themselves mere misery; and the satisfaction arising from the indulgence of them is little more than relief from that misery; whereas the temper of compassion and benevolence is itself delightful; and the indulgence of it, by doing good, affords new positive delight and enjoyment.[4]

John Stuart Mill called attention to the fact that conscience, the "internal sanction" of morality, generated inherently painful remorse or guilt when violated. He wrote that it was "a feeling in our own mind; a pain, more or less intense, attendant on a violation of duty, which in properly cultivated moral natures rises, in the more serious cases, into shrinking from it as an impossibility."[5] Mill regarded conscience, however, as "not innate but acquired,"[6] but as involving inherently agreeable feelings when followed and inherently disagreeable feelings when violated. Conscience needed to be cultivated in the right direction and supplemented by other morally virtuous motives, such as natural sympathy and fellow feeling. Mill believed that such moral motives and the activities issuing from them were inherently enjoyable as they occurred, as well as being productive of future enjoyment for all affected by them. He made the strange remark, incompatible with hedonism on the surface, that virtue and other goods were desirable as ends in themselves. He wrote that the utilitarian doctrine maintained "not only that virtue is to be desired, but that it is to be desired disinterestedly, for itself,"[7] and that:

> The ingredients of happiness are very various, and each of them is desirable in itself, and not merely when considered as swelling an aggregate. The principle of utility does not mean that any given pleasure, as music, for instance, or any given exemption from pain, as for example health, is to be looked upon as means to a collective something termed happiness, and to be desired on that account. They are desired and desirable in and for themselves; besides being means, they are part of the end. Virtue, according to the utilitarian doctrine, is not naturally and originally part of the end, but it is capable of becoming so; and in those who love it disinterestedly it has become so, and is desired and cherished, not as a means to happiness, but as a part of their happiness.[8]

Was Mill abandoning his qualitative hedonism in stating that virtue, music, health, and even power, fame, and money were ends in themselves, or integral parts of happiness itself? Is there a nonhedonistic concept of happiness functioning here? G. E. Moore was fully convinced that Mill was uttering "contemptible nonsense."[9] Yet Mill was not being stupid or inconsistent at all, if we look more carefully at what he is saying. First of all, he clearly says that all desirable things "are desirable either for the pleasure inherent in themselves, or as a means to the promotion of pleasure and the prevention of pain."[10] In the second place, he makes it clear that moral virtue is *both* inherently pleasant *and* productive of general happiness. Finally, he explains that he uses the expression desirable "for its own sake" to *mean* that something is *inherently* pleasant. He tells us that "those who desire virtue for its own sake desire it either because the consciousness of it is a pleasure, or because the consciousness of being without it is a pain, or for both reasons united";[11] and that "to think of an object as desirable (unless for the sake of its consequences) and to think of it as pleasant are one and the same thing."[12] We can quarrel with Mill's equating of "desirable in itself" with "pleasant" if we want to, but what he meant to say is clear enough. When Mill says that virtue, health, power, and fame are desirable as ends or for their own sake, he means merely that they are inherently enjoyable; and this is perfectly consistent with his hedonism. "Inherently enjoyable" here means that the pleasure we derive from them is a *simultaneous* accompaniment of their possession, and not merely a future product of it.

Now, it would be perfectly legitimate for quantitative hedonism to recognize, with qualitative hedonism, that many human activities and experiences do not merely aim at future pleasure, but are inherently enjoyable, or simultaneously accompanied by agreeable feelings. For example, Epicurus wrote, "In all other occupations the fruit comes painfully after completion, but in philosophy pleasure goes hand in hand with knowledge; for enjoyment does not follow comprehension, but comprehension and enjoyment are simultaneous."[13] Philosophy is not, as Epicurus suggested, unique in this respect, for many experiences and activities are inherently enjoyable. What the quantitative hedonist could not do, however, is to recognize a difference *in quality* or in *intrinsic worth* between the pleasures of virtuous activity and those of "sensory indulgence." In our kind of world, the localized pleasures of sexual promiscuity, eating, drinking, and tactile stimulation, may have long-range liabilities; but *Brave New World* shows us a possible ordering of society in which they do not tend to produce a preponderance of pain over pleasure in the long run. The quantitative hedonist must, as we saw, hold that if the liabilities are removed and sheer quantity of enjoyment is equal, they are just as good as, and may be substituted for poetry, art, creativity, truth, interpersonal intimacy, and moral activity, without loss of intrinsic worth. This replaceability thesis is, however, inimical to the assumptions of qualitative hedonism. *Brave New World* seems to present a fair example of a quantitatively hedonistic utopia, but it is not a qualitatively hedonistic paradise. Most of the "higher" nonlocalized varieties of agreeable feeling are almost totally lacking. If the qualitative hedonist is right about the intrinsic superiority in value of certain of the nonlocalized pleasures such as those of knowledge, interpersonal intimacy, and effortful moral activity, then these cannot be replaced without loss of intrinsic worth by the pleasures of the feelies, scent organs, *soma,* and sex without love, which are enjoyed by the Brave New Worlders. In both quality and intrinsic worth the former pleasures are different from the latter, even if the quantity of the latter is the same or even greater.

Anticipations of Qualitative Hedonism in the History of Philosophy

Probably the most insuperable objection to qualitative hedonism is that if it should turn out to be true that pleasures differ qualitatively as well as quantitatively, practically all the textbooks in ethics that have appeared in over a century would have to be drastically rewritten. A few recent journal articles have defended Mill,[14] but most critical as well as textbook discussions of him have assumed that his qualitative hedonism was unintelligible, confused, or downright mistaken. Either Mill himself did not know what he was talking about, or he abandoned hedonism altogether and became a pluralist who failed to recognize or acknowledge his own pluralism; so most of his expositors and critics maintain. Qualitative hedonism today stands just about where it was more than a hundred years ago when Mill introduced it into modern philosophy. Yet Mill was not the first thinker to suggest that pleasures might differ *in kind* as well as in degree, duration, and long-range effects. Anticipations of at least some of the central theses of qualitative hedonism are plentiful in Greek philosophy, especially in the writings of Plato and Aristotle. Neither would have regarded himself as giving the qualitative hedonistic answer to the question of the nature of the good life for man, but they came very close to it at times, as we shall see. In their treatment of the topics of pleasure and pain they anticipated all the linguistic and psychological theses of qualitative hedonism that we have sketched, and they developed as well a profound general psychology of pleasure and pain upon which a modern qualitative hedonist can readily build. Spinoza also anticipated some of the systematic features of qualitative hedonism, though he would not have regarded himself as a qualitative hedonist.

Although the suggestions that they made along these lines are not as fully or consistently developed as we might hope, nevertheless, Plato, Aristotle, and, later, Spinoza anticipated the linguistic and psychological theses that "pleasure" and "pain" do not refer to single qualities of feeling, that some of these qualities of feeling differ in kind from other such qualities called by the same name. They suggest that difference in kind adds up to a difference in intrinsic worth, and they even hint at the thesis of nonreplaceability that is central to qualitative hedonism.

Not only quantitative hedonists have assumed that "pleasure" refers to a single quality of feeling. Even such opponents of quantitative hedonism as G. E. Moore have shared this assumption while opposing the normative features of the theory of hedonism. Moore treated "pleasure" the same way that he treated "good," as the name for a single, simple, unanalyzable indefinable, intuited quality. He wrote:

> Suppose a man says "I am pleased"; and suppose that is not a lie or a mistake but the truth. Well, if it is true, what does that mean? It means that his mind, a certain definite mind, distinguished by certain definite marks from all others, has at this moment a certain definite feeling called pleasure. "Pleased" *means* nothing but having pleasure, and though we may be more pleased or less pleased, and even, we may admit for the present, have one or another kind of pleasure; yet in so far as it is pleasure we have, whether there be more or less of it, and whether it be of one kind or another, what we have is one definite thing, absolutely indefinable, some one thing that is the same in all the various degrees and in all the various kinds of it that there may be. We may be able to say how it is related to other things: that, for example, it is in the mind, that it causes desire, that we are conscious of it, etc. etc. We can, I say, describe its relations to other things, but define it we can *not.*[15]

Moore goes on to tell us that "pleasure is pleasure and nothing else whatever,"[16] and he rejects Mill's qualitative hedonism on the grounds of the linguistic thesis that " 'pleasant' must, if words are to have any meaning at all, denote some one quality common to all the things that are pleasant."[17] Many thinkers have not accepted Moore's view, however, as we shall see.

"Pleasure" and "Pain" as Abstract Class Concepts

In his dialogue *Philebus,* which is his most mature and definitive treatise on hedonism, Plato made the suggestion that "pleasure" was not a name for a single intuited quality of feeling at all. It was instead a generic or abstract class concept, like color, or figure, he proposed. Plato developed the dialogue as follows:

SOCRATES   But pleasure I know to be manifold, and with her, as I was just now saying, we must begin, and consider what her nature

84

is. She has one name, and therefore you would imagine that she is one; and yet surely she takes the most varied and even unlike forms. For do we not say that the intemperate has pleasure, and that the temperate has pleasure in his very temperance,—that the fool is pleased when he is full of foolish fancies and hopes, and that the wise man has pleasure in his wisdom? and how foolish would any one be who affirmed that all these opposite pleasures are severally alike!

PROTARCHUS   Why, Socrates, they are opposed in so far as they spring from opposite sources, but they are not in themselves opposite. For must not pleasure be of all things most absolutely like pleasure,—that is, like itself?

SOCRATES   Yes, my good friend, just as colour is like colour;—in so far as colours are colours, there is no difference between them; and yet we all know that black is not only unlike, but even absolutely opposed to white: or again, a figure is like figure, for all figures are comprehended under one class; and yet particular figures may be absolutely opposed to one another, and there is an infinite diversity of them. And we might find similar examples in many other things; therefore do not rely upon this argument, which would go to prove the unity of the most extreme opposites. And I suspect that we shall find a similar opposition among pleasures.[18]

In his attempted refutation of Mill's qualitative hedonism, Moore did discuss the analogy of "pleasure" with "color," but he rejected the analogy on the grounds that "if you say 'pleasure,' you must mean 'pleasure': you must mean some one thing common to all different 'pleasures,' some one thing, which may exist in different degrees, but which cannot differ in *kind*."[19] Yet this linguistic thesis is precisely what is called into question by qualitative hedonism, and it is question-begging merely to reintroduce it in refutation of qualitative hedonism. If the analogy Plato suggested is correct, there is no *one* concretely intuited quality of experience called "pleasure" any more than there is one concretely intuited quality of experience called "color." Both are abstract class concepts, and the members of the respective classes can and do differ in kind as well as in degree. Black and white are concretely intuited qualities of experience, just as are the pleasures of knowledge and the pleasures of eating peppermint ice cream; but we never directly intuit pure color as such or pure pleasure as such. The class of pleasures is the class of feelings we like and ordinarily desire to sustain and cultivate, just as the class of colors is the class of visual sensations that vary with changes of frequency of light. Though Plato did not present the concept of pain as generic, it also should be treated as an abstract class concept rather than as the name of a single directly intuited quality of feeling. Pain is the class of all those multifarious feelings that we dislike and ordinarily desire to eliminate or avoid, and pains differ as much from one another as black differs from white. We wish to eliminate and avoid the concrete disagreeable feelings of grief or despair, just as we wish to eliminate and avoid the concrete disagreeable feelings of a pin prick or a burn. But grief is as unlike a pin prick as black is unlike white. Concrete intuited qualities can differ in kind, while still belonging to the same abstract class. Neglect of this possibility leads only to the dogmatic assertion that "pleasure is pleasure" and "pain is pain" and with it the rejection of qualitative hedonism.

"Pleasure" and "Pain" as Species Concepts

If pleasures and pains differ qualitatively, then there are different species of pleasure and pain, just as there are different species of color and figure. We never directly experience pure pleasure or pure pain as such, just as we never directly experience pure color or pure size or shape. We do directly experience particular instances or species of color, such as red or blue, and particular species of shape, such as circles and triangles. We also directly experience particular species of pleasure and pain, but how are they to be identified and distinguished from one another? They are identified and distinguished in all instances by mentioning other specific causes, activities, or qualities of experience with which they are associated—the pleasures of inquiring, the pleasure of contemplation, the pleasure of intimacy, the pleasure of eating apple pie, the pleasure of a back rub, the pleasure of sexual orgasm—or the pain of grief, the pain of guilt, the pain of appendicitis, the pain of a bee sting. In this list of examples, some of the nonaffective properties mentioned are the *causes* of their associated pleasures and pains, and some are their intentional *objects*. This is an important distinction.

For the theory of qualitative hedonism, intentional pleasures and pains that must be identified and differentiated by their intentional objects are extremely important and will receive the most attention. I am not maintaining here, however, that all species of pleasure and pain involve intentionality, though *most* of them do. For the present it seems best to leave open the question whether *all* pleasures and pains in the concrete involve intentionality and are conceptually and experientially inseparable from their intended objects. There do seem to be some pleasures not bound to specific objects, such as a general joy in life or the objectless bliss of some mystics' nirvana. If there are such objectless pleasures, they cannot be identified and distinguished by reference to objects, as can intentional pleasures. The same is true of such seemingly objectless pains as genuinely "free-floating" anxiety and irrational fear, lacking all focus. Objectless pleasures and pains have to be distinguished conceptually from one another either in terms of their causes or sources, the bliss of nirvana being the kind of pleasure that results from certain techniques of meditation, or in terms of behavioral effects, such as the exuberant activity which is a consequence of a general joy in life.

Intentional pleasures and pains may be distinguished from one another by their objects, that is, those nonaffective properties of experience from which they are inseparable. Intentional pleasures and pains are like specific desires, which are always desires *for* something, and which can be distinguished from one another only as we specify what they are desires for.[20] Concepts of this sort are called "intentional" concepts in current literature on the philosophy of mind.[21] Intentional concepts are those which always require an object, which are logically incomplete and indefinite without one. "Desire" is always desire for something in the concrete. "Consciousness" is almost always consciousness of something in the concrete, though mystics speak of pure, objectless consciousness as such. Similarly, intentional pleasures in the concrete are always pleasures of a certain kind, having a certain object; and intentional pains are always pains of a certain kind, having a certain object. Concrete instances falling under these concepts cannot be identified in experience, thought, or imagination in total isolation from some intended object; and they cannot be distinguished *fully* from one another except by including their intended object. This does not mean that the concrete referents of such concepts cannot otherwise be differentiated *at all,* as is sometimes assumed, for they can be partially distinguished in locus, in time, in duration, and in strength from one another.[22] But they cannot be *fully* identified or distinguished except in connection with their intended object. C. D. Broad was in effect suggesting that pleasure and pain were always intentional concepts when he wrote:

> We must begin by remarking that it is logically impossible that an experience should have no characteristic except hedonic quality. It is as clear that no experience could be *merely* pleasant or painful as that nothing could be black or white without also having some shape and some size. Consequently the hedonist can neither produce nor conceive an instance of an experience which was just pleasant or painful and nothing more; and so he cannot judge by direct inspection that hedonic quality is necessary and sufficient to determine intrinsic value. He is therefore reduced to

reflecting on instances in which hedonic quality is combined with non-hedonic characteristics.[23]

We have developed the linguistic hypotheses that the concepts of "pleasure" and "pain," considered in the abstract, function as generic or class concepts; and that considered in the concrete, they usually function as intentional concepts. The same is true of related concepts like "desire" and "consciousness." All these concepts have both generic and specific meaning. If they are intentional in most of their specific senses, this means that most concrete species of these classes are not fully distinguishable from one another or identifiable in experience, thought, or imagination in total isolation from their intended objects, or in total isolation from other properties of experience or predicates of thought. If this is the case, we now have a *logical* reason for rejecting the replaceability thesis of quantitative hedonism. The pleasures of contemplation are not replaceable by equally prolonged and intense pleasures of copulation. The two kinds of pleasure are not even adequately identifiable if their objects are eliminated from thought and experience. Each distinctive concrete quality of intentional agreeable feeling is always associated with its distinctive object, and is fully available to us in immediate experience, in thought, and in imagination, only in conjunction with that object. Qualitative hedonism now has a linguistic or logical foundation, for intentional pleasure in the concrete or specific sense is always logically inextricable from other qualities of experience and thought. If we are to have those distinctive pleasures, we must also always have their distinctive intended objects—no substitutions allowed. Aristotle seems to have anticipated this linguistic feature of qualitative hedonism when he wrote, "Perhaps pleasures differ in kind; for those derived from noble sources are different from those derived from base sources, and one cannot get the pleasure of the just man without being just, nor that of the musical man without being musical, and so on."[24] He

here identifies source and object, just as they are often exten-
sionally the same.

Aristotle's view seems to have been that the intended object
or source of pleasure was some activity, in the broad sense of
"activity" as "the actualization of a potentiality." Distinctive
kinds of pleasures are associated with different activities and
are derivable only from, or at least in conjunction with, those
activities. Aristotle explains:

> For this reason pleasures seem, too, to differ in kind. For things
> different in kind are, we think, completed by different things (we
> see this to be true both of natural objects and of things produced
> by art, e.g. animals, trees, a painting, a sculpture, a house, an
> implement); and, similarly, we think that activities differing in
> kind are completed by things different in kind. Now the activities
> of thought differ from those of the senses, and both differ
> among themselves, in kind; so, therefore, do the pleasures that
> complete them.
>
> This may be seen, too, from the fact that each of the pleasures
> is bound up with the activity it completes.[25]

The intentional nature of specific pleasure and pain concepts also seems to have been anticipated by Spinoza, who developed the thesis in these words:

> The pleasure, which arises from, say, the object A, involves the
> nature of that object A, and the pleasure, which arises from the
> object B, involves the nature of the object B; wherefore these two
> pleasurable emotions are by nature different, inasmuch as the
> causes whence they arise are by nature different. So again the
> emotion of pain, which arises from one object, is by nature dif-
> ferent from the pain arising from another object, and, similarly,
> in the case of love, hatred, hope, fear, vacillation, etc.
>
> Thus, there are necessarily as many kinds of pleasure, pain,
> love, hatred, etc., as there are kinds of objects whereby we are
> affected.[26]

Spinoza explores in some detail the connection between pleasure, pain, and various virtuous and nonvirtuous motives and

dispositions. Anyone interested in the theme that virtue is its own reward and vice its own punishment should read his *Ethics*, especially Parts III and IV.

Qualitative hedonists agree with Aristotle that "each kind of pleasure is bound up with the activity it completes," and with Spinoza that pleasure involves the nature of its object; and the suggestion is that the bond is both experiential and logical or conceptual. Even Mill anticipated intentionality of pleasure when he suggested that the objects of our happiness are an integral part of that happiness. We can never concretely experience a specific kind of pleasure in total isolation from its intended object, and we can never even think of or imagine a specific kind of pleasure in total isolation from its intended object. Consider, for example, the case of eating a spoonful of sugar. The sweetness of the sugar is pleasant. The sweetness of sugar is both the source and the intentional object of the pleasure, but are there really *two* completely distinguishable qualities of experience here? Is there one quite distinct quality of sweetness, and another quite distinct quality of pleasantness? No, it seems that the sweetness *is* the pleasantness in the sense that it is that concrete quality of feeling which we like and desire to sustain and repeat. We do not experience two clearly separable qualities. The distinctive pleasure of tasting the sweetness of sugar cannot be had in experience, in thought, or in imagination in total isolation from the taste of sweetness of sugar, and this is true of all our intentional pleasures in the concrete. They are not available to us except through their intended objects.

Before we leave the topic of the intentionality of pleasures and pains, a final word must be said about the relation between the sources and the intentional objects of such feelings. The source of a pleasure is its cause, as for example hearing good news is the source of my enjoyment of it; but the good news heard is the object of that enjoyment. Usually there is a close relation between source and intentional object, but they are logically distinct and often actually separated. In speaking causal language we are talking about the actualities of the real world, whereas intentional objects involve phenomenology alone. That is, they involve merely the way things are presented to us in experience itself. We saw in our treatment of electrode-stimulated universes of experience in Chapter 3 that there is no necessary relation between the cause and the phenomenal object of a pleasure. The pleasures of sexual intercourse are normally generated by real sexual intercourse, but they may also be generated by electronic stimulation of the septal region of the brain. It would have been a poor defense of qualitative hedonism to have argued that the real world is to be preferred to an electronically stimulated universe of experience because intentional pleasures are not available to us except through their normal *sources,* for the most that can be claimed for intentional pleasures is that they are not available to us except through their intentional *objects,* that is, those nonaffective properties of phenomenal experience from which they are experientially and conceptually inseparable. But intentional objects of pleasure don't have to *exist* in the real world, though often they do. If by electronic brain stimulation, the phenomenal taste of peppermint ice cream could be richly reproduced, then we would not need to eat real peppermint ice cream to experience just that form of enjoyment. The same thing is true in principle of all other intentional pleasures (or pains). Normally, however, the most efficient way to experience these forms of enjoyment is to stay in touch with the real world.

Relations between Desires, Pleasures, and Pains

We have identified the generic class of "pleasure" as the set of all feelings we desire or wish to sustain or cultivate, and the generic class of "pain" as the set of all feelings we wish or desire to eliminate and avoid. It is possible, however, that this move is logically circular; for the notion of desire might be synonymous with the notion of pleasure. We might thus be saying that the class "pleasure" is the set of all feelings we are *pleased* to sustain or cultivate, and the class "pain" is the set of all feelings we are *pained* to sustain or cultivate. This charge of circularity can be met fully only if we further explore the notion of "desire" and its possible connections with notions of "pleasure" and "pain."

There is much to be said for the behavioristic contention that a desire for something is merely a tendency to act to get that thing. The word "merely" is the troublesome thing here, however. In addition to being tendencies to act, desires are also psychic tensions toward or away from various objects. These tensions may be satisfied immediately in the present as well as being future-oriented toward more of the same. Such immediate or directly present satisfaction we call a "liking," but a liking is not yet another pleasant feeling in response to a given pleasant feeling. To like a given agreeable feeling is simply to find that it immediately satisfies or positively fulfills a given desire. As the term "desire" is here used, a desire is a tension or attraction toward (or away from) an object either present or future, not simply a tension toward a future object. Psychologists tell us that some desires are unconscious, and others fully conscious. A conscious desire is a felt inner tension or attraction toward or away from some object of experience, thought, or imagination. Such desires or tensions may vary considerably in intensity and duration and may conflict with one another. Though conscious desires may resemble pleasures in some ways, nevertheless, the two are not identical. "Desire" and "pleasure" are not synonyms. The thing that gives initial plausibility to the charge of circularity is that it is true that some desires are pleasant, but it does not follow from this that a feeling is a desire if and only if it is pleasant. To say that some desires are pleasant is to say that some (but not all) desires have integral feeling tones that we like and can and do normally desire to sustain and repeat. We can, and sometimes do, have desires as objects of desire. Unless excruciatingly intense, sexual desire is an inherently pleasant desire. This is the whole point of standing on the corner watching all the girls go by. Sexual desire is itself inherently enjoyable, even if there is no prospect that it can be "satisfied" by actual possession of the girl or the boy, as the case might be. Many desires, when not overly intense, are inherently pleasant. As John Hospers puts it, "The state of desire is not necessarily painful or even unpleasant. Acute hunger is painful, but a mild hunger, carrying with it anticipations of satisfaction may be quite pleasant. It is not true that every satisfaction of desire presupposes a previous state of dissatisfaction."[27]

Though the inherent pleasantness of some desires lends initial plausibility to the claim that "desire" means "pleasant," the fact that *other* desires are inherently painful constitutes conclusive evidence that the two concepts are not synonyms, and that no circularity is involved in our generic definitions of "pleasure" and "pain." Actually, more attention has been given historically to the inherent painfulness of some desires than to the inherent pleasurableness of others. In his earlier dialogues, such as the *Gorgias,* Plato seems to have accepted the contention that "all wants or desires are painful."[28] In later dialogues, however, he seems to maintain only that only our most sudden and intense desires are painful and that moderate or modest desire is not painful at all.[29] Nevertheless, Plato's earlier contention that all desire as such is intrinsically painful has had tremendous historical influence. The Stoics accepted the thesis and urged the complete elimination or suppression of all desire. Buddhism independently originated it and bases much of its world renunciation upon it. Schopenhauer accepted it, along with the thesis that all pleasure results from the satisfaction of painful desire, and developed one of the most pessimistic philosophies ever worked out. But the thesis is false, as are all gross oversimplifications. Some desires are indeed inherently painful, but some are not. In neither case does "x is desired" mean simply that "x is pleasant." Thus, it is not logically circular to define "pleasure" in the generic sense as "feelings we like and normally desire to sustain and cultivate."

C. D. Broad correctly explained the difference between desire and pleasure and pain:

> Sidgwick points out that desire is not usually a painful experience, unless it be very intense and be continually frustrated. No doubt desire is an unrestful state, in the sense that it tends to make us change our present condition. It shares this characteristic with genuine pain. But the difference is profound. When I feel aversion to a present pain I simply try to get rid of it. When I feel the unrest of desire for a certain object I do not simply try to get rid of the uneasiness; I try to get that particular object.[30]

The claim that the generic meaning of "pleasure" is "the set of all feelings we desire or wish to sustain or cultivate" thus does not mean "the set of all feelings we are pleased to sustain or cultivate." Rather it means "the set of all feelings for which we have a psychic tension or attraction," and no circularity is involved. Similarly, "pain" in the generic sense means "the set of all feelings against which we have a psychic tension or aversion."

Is it true that pleasure results only from the satisfaction of desire, whether desire be painful or not? This thesis has had great historical influence, but it too is false. And it should not be confused with the (analytically) true thesis that when pleasant feelings do occur, we do normally desire to sustain and repeat them. This analytically true thesis, in turn, should not be confused with the false claim of Schopenhauer's pessimism that all pleasure results from the satisfaction of painful desire. Some pleasures occur without having been preceded by desires at all—we do have "pleasant surprises," such as the unexpected and undesired odor of honeysuckle in the air on a summer evening. When these pleasant surprises occur, we do normally wish to sustain them, at least for a while. We may tire of such feelings eventually, but when all liking and tensions to sustain and repeat them have run their course, then they cease to be pleasures. It remains true, however, that they were pleasures as long as the liking and positive attraction were there. Without being preceded by desire, they create a present attraction and liking which eventually terminate. Plato mentioned such pleasant odors as examples of those pleasures "which are very great and have no antecedent pains; they come in a moment, and when they depart leave no pain behind them."[31] Finally, none of the claims of qualitative hedonism should be confused with the false claim of egoistic psychological hedonism that the only object of every desire is a pleasant feeling for oneself. We desire food, drink, companionship, and other things as well as pleasure. The intrinsic *value* of these other objects of desire may reside in some quality of pleasant feeling, but these objects are not themselves merely pleasant feelings, and we may desire these things for other people as well as for ourselves.

Having now explored some of the basic systematic features of a theory of qualitative hedonism, we must now turn to some still unanswered questions about such a position.

5

Some Unanswered Questions

Having explored some of the systematic features of qualitative hedonism, we must now deal with some important and still unanswered questions. Is qualitative hedonism really a disguised form of pluralism? How can we tell which pleasures are intrinsically better, and which pains are intrinsically worse, than others? What is the qualitatively hedonistic conception of happiness and the good life? Finally, can a theory of action and obligation be developed from qualitative hedonism?

The Distinction between Qualitative Hedonism and Pluralism

Ever since the publication of *Utilitarianism,* the suspicion has persisted among Mill's countless critics that qualitative hedonism is really pluralism in disguise, and that as such it is actually a complete abandonment of hedonism. If it is possible for some intrinsic good to be quantitatively less pleasant than, yet better than some other good, is this not because the independent value of some other intrinsic good besides pleasure is added to the worth of the pleasure in the former case? And does this not concede that other things besides pleasures have intrinsic worth? Was not Mill deceiving himself and others in continuing to regard himself as a hedonist at all? These extremely serious questions must be answered in some way if qualitative hedonism is to be defended.

Hedonic and Nonhedonic Pluralism

In Chapter 1, we defined pluralism as the theory that other things besides pleasure are intrinsically good. The difficulty that many have had in seeing a real distinction between hedonism and pluralism rests in part upon the fact that, historically, pluralism has been maintained in two distinct forms, one of which is obviously closer to qualitative hedonism than the other. We shall call these *nonhedonic pluralism* and *hedonic pluralism,* and we shall show that qualitative hedonism does differ significantly from both and is an independent alternative to them. Nonhedonic pluralism is the theory that other things besides pleasure are intrinsically good *in complete isolation from* pleasure, and that other things besides pain are intrinsically bad *in complete isolation from* pain. Hedonic pluralism is the theory that though other things have no intrinsic worth in complete isolation from pleasure, nevertheless other things combine with pleasure to form wholes which may be "organic wholes" and which are of far greater value than the pleasure component all by itself would be; and that though other things are not intrinsically bad in complete isolation from pain, nevertheless other things combine with pain to form wholes which may be "organic wholes" and which are of far greater disvalue than the pain component alone would be. The hedonic pluralist may hold that in some cases, pleasure combines with other properties to form organic wholes which are intrinsically bad rather than intrinsically good.

Since both forms of pluralism were seemingly espoused by G. E. Moore, in different stages of his intellectual development, we shall allow him to be the principal spokesman for both forms of the theory. We shall also show that qualitative hedonism differs significantly from both forms of the theory as Moore developed them. In his *Principia Ethica,* published in 1903, Moore subscribed to a nonhedonic form of pluralism, but apparently he later abandoned it in favor of a hedonic form of pluralism, which appears in his *Ethics,* published in 1912.

In *Principia Ethica,* Moore maintained that pleasure is one intrinsic good, but not the only one, and that other things were intrinsically good in complete isolation from all agreeable feeling. He indirectly concedes the intrinsic worth of pleasure in saying that "the doctrine that pleasure, *among other things,* is good as an end, is not Hedonism; and I shall not dispute its truth."[1] But Moore went on to assert that other things besides pleasure were good as ends or intrinsic goods.

> By far the most valuable things, which we can know or can imagine, are certain states of consciousness, which may be roughly described as the pleasures of human intercourse and the enjoyment of beautiful objects. No one, probably, who has asked himself the question, has ever doubted that personal affection and the appreciation of what is beautiful in Art or Nature, are good in themselves; nor, if we consider strictly what things are worth having *purely for their own sakes,* does it appear probable that any one will think that anything else has *nearly* so great a value as the things which are included under these two heads. I have myself urged in Chap. III, (Part 50), that the mere existence of what is beautiful does appear to have *some* intrinsic value; but I regard it as indubitable that Prof. Sidgwick was so far right, in the view there discussed, that such mere existence of what is beautiful

99

so small as to be negligible, in comparison with that which attaches to the *consciousness* of beauty.[2]

Now, in his *Principia Ethica,* Moore did develop and employ his principle of "organic wholes," upon which his later theory of hedonic pluralism was built. But he nevertheless maintained in this earlier work that some things besides pleasure had intrinsic worth, however small, in total isolation from pleasure; and that some things had intrinsic disvalue, however small, in total isolation from pain. These two points need to be further explored. His definition of the principle of "organic wholes," or "organic unities" was "that the intrinsic value of a whole is neither identical with nor proportional to the sum of the value of its parts."[3] Although Moore used this concept in connection with pleasure and pain in *Principia Ethica,* saying, for example, that the enjoyment of beauty was of far greater intrinsic worth than pure enjoyment or pure beauty in isolation from each other, he nevertheless was upholding a nonhedonic form of pluralism in this work. He maintained that beauty, for example, did have *some* intrinsic value, however small, in total isolation from all actual and possible enjoyment of it; and that ugliness did have some intrinsic disvalue, however small, in total isolation from all actual and possible frustration by it. Pleasure and pain were not necessary ingredients in intrinsically good and bad wholes. Moore developed this point as follows, arguing against the hedonist Sidgwick's claims that nothing has intrinsic worth except in relation to some sentient enjoyment of it, and that we never have duties to actualize any unenjoyed goods.

> Let us imagine one world exceedingly beautiful. Imagine it as beautiful as you can; put into it whatever on this earth you most admire—mountains, rivers, the sea; trees, and sunsets, stars and moon. Imagine these all combined in the most exquisite proportions, so that no one thing jars against another, but each contrib-

utes to increase the beauty of the whole. And then imagine the
ugliest world you can possibly conceive. Imagine it simply one
heap of filth, containing everything that is most disgusting to us,
for whatever reason, and the whole, as far as may be, without one
redeeming feature. Such a pair of worlds we are entitled to compare: they fall within Prof. Sidgwick's meaning, and the comparison is highly relevant to it. The only thing we are not entitled to
imagine is that any human being ever has or ever, by any possibility, *can,* live in either, can ever see and enjoy the beauty of the
one or hate the foulness of the other. Well, even so, supposing
them quite apart from any possible contemplation by human
beings; still, is it irrational to hold that it is better that the beautiful world should exist, than the one which is ugly? Would it not
be well, in any case, to do what we could to produce it rather than
the other? Certainly I cannot help thinking that it would; and I
hope that some may agree with me in this extreme instance. The
instance is extreme.[4]

I admit, of course, that our beautiful world would be better still,
if there were human beings in it to contemplate and enjoy its
beauty. But that admission makes nothing against my point. If it
be once admitted that the beautiful world *in itself* is better than
the ugly, then it follows, that however many beings may enjoy it,
and however much better their enjoyment may be than it is itself,
yet its mere existence adds something to the goodness of the
whole: it is not only a means to our end, but also itself a part
thereof.[5]

The fact that Moore uses the principle of organic wholes in
connection with pleasure and pain in *Principia Ethica* still does
not mean that he is a hedonic pluralist, as we have defined the
term, in this earlier work. As the "beautiful world" and "ugly
world" illustrations show, he is clearly a nonhedonic pluralist
who holds that some things have intrinsic worth in total isolation from pleasure, and that some things have intrinsic disvalue
in total isolation from disagreeable feeling.

The usual form of pluralism[6] is the nonhedonic variety. In
trying to decide whether we are pluralists or hedonists, we are

usually expected to contemplate the worth of various "pluralistic goods" in total isolation from the enjoyment of them and then ascertain whether we would deem them worthy of existing, experiencing, cultivating, or promoting for their own sake. This procedure is just the reverse of the one we followed in Chapter 3, in which we tried to contemplate the worth of pleasure in near if not total isolation from such pluralistic goods as freedom, interpersonal intimacy, beauty, art, creativity, knowledge, truth, and moral virtue and activity. When the procedure is reversed, and we ask whether we would attribute any intrinsic worth to these things *assuming that we got no satisfaction or agreeable feeling from them whatsoever,* we have a powerful hedonistic argument *against* at least the nonhedonic form of pluralism. The qualitative hedonist is fully convinced by the claim that the pluralistic goods have no intrinsic worth in absolute isolation from all feelings of satisfaction in them. We shall see that even Moore finally concluded that he was probably wrong about the beautiful and ugly world examples and that very likely nothing has intrinsic value or disvalue in total isolation from pleasure or pain.

In the next chapter, we shall pay close attention to problems of methodology in ethics, but for now let us suggest that the final appeal seems to be to the intuitive preferences or judgment of people who understand ethical questions clearly and reflect upon them deeply. Many such thinkers who have considered the nonhedonic form of pluralism, who have understood clearly and reflected deeply upon the question of whether anything has intrinsic worth in total isolation from all actual and possible satisfaction, have come to negative conclusions. But since the theory of qualitative hedonism has never been very well understood, and since authorities may be cited on both sides of this controversial issue, we cannot settle the matter by appeal to thinkers of the past; we must make our own enlightened judgment. We may, however, find it helpful, clarifying, and enlightening to see how the point has been expressed by a few prominent philosophers who have concluded that nothing should be desired or chosen for its own sake in total separation from all qualities of satisfaction or agreeable feeling. Even the G. E. Moore of the *Ethics* seemingly came to this position; but centuries before him Plato, through his spokesman Socrates, reached the same negative conclusion. Plato, who located intrinsic good for man in the "mixed life" of pleasure plus other things, such as wisdom, could not accept pleasure alone, *or anything else in total isolation from pleasure,* as an intrinsic good. A life of wisdom totally devoid of all pleasure would never be chosen by anyone, it is concluded near the end of the following profound discussion in Plato's *Philebus:*

SOCRATES   Now let us part off the life of pleasure from the life of wisdom, and pass them in review.

PROTARCHUS   How do you mean?

SOCRATES   Let there be no wisdom in the life of pleasure, nor any pleasure in the life of wisdom, for if either of them is the chief good, it cannot be supposed to want anything, but if either is shown to want anything, then it cannot really be the chief good.

PROTARCHUS   Impossible. . . .

SOCRATES   Would you choose, Protarchus, to live all your life long in the enjoyment of the greatest pleasures?

PROTARCHUS   Certainly I should.

SOCRATES   Would you consider that there was still anything wanting to you if you had Perfect pleasure?

PROTARCHUS   Certainly not.

SOCRATES   Reflect; would you not want wisdom and intelligence and forethought, and similar qualities? Would you not at any rate want sight?

PROTARCHUS   Why should I? Having pleasure I should have all things. . . .

SOCRATES   But if you had neither mind, nor memory, nor knowledge, nor true opinion, you would in the first place be utterly ignorant of whether you were pleased or not, because you would be entirely devoid of intelligence.

PROTARCHUS   Certainly.

SOCRATES   And similarly, if you had no memory you would not recognize that you had ever been pleased, nor would the slightest recollection of the pleasure which you feel at any moment remain with you; and if you had not true opinion you would not think that you were pleased when you were; and if you had no power of calculation you would not be able to calculate on future pleasure, and your life would be the life, not of a man, but of an oyster or "pulmo marinus." Could this be otherwise?

PROTARCHUS   No.

SOCRATES   But is such a life eligible?

PROTARCHUS   I cannot answer you, Socrates; the argument has taken away from me the power of speech.

SOCRATES   We must keep up our spirits;—let us now take the life of mind and examine it in turn.

PROTARCHUS   And what is this life of mind?

SOCRATES   I want to know whether any one of us would consent to live, having wisdom and mind and knowledge and memory of all things, but having no sense of pleasure or pain, and wholly unaffected by these and the like feelings?

PROTARCHUS   Neither life, Socrates, appears eligible to me, or is likely, as I should imagine, to be chosen by any one else.

SOCRATES   What would you say, Protarchus, to both of these in one, or to one that was made out of the union of the two?

PROTARCHUS   Out of the union, that is, of pleasure with mind and wisdom?

SOCRATES   Yes, that is the life which I mean.

PROTARCHUS   There can be no difference of opinion; not some but all would surely choose this third rather than either of the other two, and in addition to them.[7]

Plato, who comes out here as a hedonic pluralist, has not been alone in rejecting nonhedonic pluralism. Many contemporary thinkers who have considered the question whether the pluralistic goods in total isolation from all satisfaction have any intrinsic worth have also come to negative conclusions. These people would also probably classify themselves as hedonic pluralists, but they clearly reject nonhedonic pluralism. In discussing the intrinsic worth of knowledge, and the enjoyable fulfillment of what he calls "the theoretic impulse," Brand Blanshard writes:

> We repeat, however, that it is not satisfaction merely that the impulse is seeking, but that which will satisfy it, namely this particular kind of light. But neither is it light merely; for what is the point of a knowledge in which one takes no satisfaction? What is sought is something which, because of its special character, fulfils the aim of the cognitive impulse, and which because of this fulfillment, satisfies. This double service of fulfilling and of satisfying is what makes knowledge good. It is also what makes anything good.[8]

Writing on the pluralistic goods, and apparently assuming the thesis of qualitative hedonism that pleasures or agreeable feelings *do* differ in quality, William K. Frankena gives this opinion of nonhedonic pluralism:

> What about hedonistic thesis (3): that nothing is intrinsically good which does not contain pleasure? If, as I suggested, we distinguish other kinds of satisfactoriness besides pleasure, then thesis (3) is not true. But the broader and somewhat similar thesis that nothing is intrinsically good unless it contains some kind of satisfactoriness seems to me to be clearly true. Thus, I think that knowledge, excellence, power, and so on, are simply cold, bare, and valueless in themselves unless they are experienced with some kind of enjoyment or satisfaction.[9]

Many clear-headed thinkers from Plato's time to our own have rejected the nonhedonic form of pluralism, though most of them would have classified themselves as hedonic pluralists rather than as qualitative hedonists. Let us see if there is a real difference between the two, or whether the suspicion that qualitative hedonism is really pluralism (now of the hedonic variety) in disguise is well founded. It might turn out that hedonic pluralism is really qualitative hedonism in disguise!

Hedonic pluralism, let us remind ourselves, is the view that although other things have no intrinsic value (or disvalue) in total isolation from pleasure (or pain), nevertheless they may combine with pleasure (or pain) to form wholes that may be "organic wholes," which are of far greater value (or disvalue) than the pleasure (or pain) component taken all by itself. Hedonic pluralism thus agrees with the rejection of the nonhedonic thesis that other things have intrinsic value or disvalue completely apart from all feelings of satisfaction or dissatisfaction. It concedes that pleasure must be at least *one* component of every intrinsic good, and pain of every intrinsic bad. Moore came at least very close to accepting this view in his *Ethics,* after decisively rejecting it in *Principia Ethica.* In his *Ethics,* he says of the thesis that "no whole can ever be intrinsically good, *unless* it contains some pleasure," that: "for my part, though I don't feel certain that this proposition *is* true, I also don't feel at all certain that it is *not* true." He further elaborates by telling us:

> There do seem to be two important characteristics, which are *common* to absolutely all intrinsic goods, though not peculiar to them. Namely (1) it does seem as if nothing can be an intrinsic good unless it contains *both* some feeling and *also* some other form of consciousness; and, as we have said before, it seems possible that amongst the feelings contained must always be some amount of pleasure. And (2) it does also seem as if every intrinsic good must be a complex whole containing a considerable variety of factors—as if, for instance, nothing so simple as pleasure by itself, however intense, could ever be any good.... It seems also to be true that nothing can be intrinsically bad, *unless* it contains some feeling.[10]

Now for the hard question: Is qualitative hedonism really hedonic pluralism in disguise? No, it clearly is not, at least in the form in which hedonic pluralism was held by Moore and perhaps by all other hedonic pluralists. Hedonic pluralism of

the Moore variety makes several assumptions that are decisively rejected by qualitative hedonism. It assumes with quantitative hedonism (1) that there is only *one* quality of feeling
called "pleasure," and *one* quality of feeling called "pain";
whereas qualitative hedonism maintains that "pleasure" refers
to *many* qualitatively distinct feelings which we like and normally wish to sustain and repeat, and that "pain" refers to an
equally wide range of qualitatively distinct feelings which we
dislike and normally wish to eliminate and avoid. Hedonic
pluralism further assumes (2) that when we are considering the
question of whether pleasure is *an* intrinsic good or pain *an*
intrinsic bad, we are contemplating the worth of merely *one*
quality of feeling. By contrast, qualitative hedonism maintains
that since pleasures are qualitatively many, their intrinsic worth
may and does vary as quality (and not merely intensity and
duration) varies—and similarly for pains and their intrinsic
disvalue. Some special type of pleasure or pain seems to be
taken as paradigmatic by hedonic pluralists, probably the localized pleasures of sex and the localized pain of the stomachache or toothache; and it would be a great contribution to
clarity if they made their paradigms explicit. For the qualitative hedonist, however, there are no paradigmatic pleasures
and pains. Again, the hedonic pluralist assumes that (3) it is
possible to *isolate totally* the feelings of pleasure and pain from
all other properties of experience, thought, and imagination;
but this claim is disputed by the qualitatively hedonistic contention that since "pleasure" and "pain" in the specific senses usually are intentional concepts, it is not possible to isolate completely or identify fully the concrete feelings they denote in
total isolation from all other properties of experience, thought,
and imagination. To apply Moore's principle of organic wholes
in the hedonically pluralistic way, we must be able to perform
each of the following operations. We must be able (a) to contemplate the value of *pure* pleasure, then (b) to contemplate the

value of some isolated nonhedonic property, then (c) contemplate the value of their conjunction in some organic whole, then (d) realize that the value of the organic whole is far greater than the value of pure pleasure or its other components taken in isolation. Unless *each* of these steps can be taken, the principle of organic wholes has no relevant application whatsoever. Now, qualitative hedonism emphatically denies that step (a) and consequently steps (c) and (d) are possible. We are never in a position to contemplate the worth of *pure* pleasure in either experience, thought, or imagination. There is no one quality of agreeable feeling that would count as pure pleasure, and intentional pleasures are not available to us in total isolation from their objects. Consequently, we are never in a position to compare the worth of pure pleasure in total isolation with the worth of pleasure in some larger organic whole, or to realize that the intrinsic worth of the latter is greater than that of the former. Consequently, the principle of organic wholes, as Moore conceived it, has no relevant application. Similar things are true of pains in isolation, and as ingredients of organic wholes. What clearer evidence is needed to show that qualitative hedonism is *not* hedonic pluralism in disguise? Hastings Rashdall, who would have considered himself to be a hedonic pluralist, was somewhat inconsistent with his own position in maintaining that "value is not a feeling, but it cannot be recognized as attributable to anything in consciousness which can excite no feeling of pleasure in its possessor. The fallacy of Hedonism lies in the attempt to estimate the value of the feeling element in abstraction from the other elements of consciousness."[11]

This "fallacy" is common to both quantitative hedonism and hedonic pluralism, but qualitative hedonism does not commit it.

It should be carefully noted that qualitative hedonism denies that we ever have access in experience, thought, or imagination to a single quality of *pure* pleasure, or a single quality of *pure* pain, in total isolation from other properties. There is no such thing as pure pleasure or pure pain. Qualitative hedonism does not deny, however, that *specific* intentional pleasures and pains always exist and must be reflected upon in relation to or conjunction with other properties. This latter point still gives room for suspicion that qualitative hedonism is really *some* form of pluralism in disguise. Now, we have shown clearly that qualitative hedonism is not nonhedonic or hedonic pluralism. Is there some form of pluralism still remaining which is really identical with qualitative hedonism? Possibly so, but it has never been clearly formulated by any pluralist, and it might consequently be of little consequence what we call it if it is clearly distinguished from quantitative hedonism, and both nonhedonic and hedonic pluralism. Thus, there might be some fourth theory which holds that (a) specific, concrete pleasures and pains differ qualitatively; (b) intentional pleasures and pains are always given in experience, thought, and imagination in conjunction with other properties; (c) these other nonhedonic properties can be experienced, thought, and imagined in isolation from pleasures and pains, however; (d) when these nonhedonic properties are so isolated, we see intuitively that they have no intrinsic worth or disvalue; (e) there is no way to tell that intentional pleasures out of context of other nonhedonic properties have more worth than pleasures in such contexts, or that intentional pains out of context of other nonhedonic properties have less disvalue than in such contexts; (f) some pleasures-in-context are intrinsically more valuable than other pleasures-in-context, and some pains-in-context are intrinsically more disvaluable than other pains-in-context; and (g) such "superior" pleasures ought to be chosen in preference to "inferior" pleasures when the latter are incompatible with the former.

Such a theory would be clearly hedonistic in its denial that other things besides (that is, in total isolation from) pleasures and pains have intrinsic value or disvalue. Is it equally hedonistic in the positive sense of affirming that *only* pleasures or pains have intrinsic value or disvalue? If this is interpreted to mean that only pleasure or pains *in total isolation* from all other properties have value or disvalue, then our theory is not positively hedonistic in this sense, since it denies the possibility of total isolation where intentionality is involved. However, it is very doubtful that any hedonist has ever meant to say that only pleasure and pain in total isolation from *all* other properties, such as experience, consciousness, or awareness, for example, have intrinsic value or disvalue. Even Moore reluctantly conceded that "it may be said that Hedonists have always meant by pleasure the consciousness of pleasure, though they have not been at pains to say so; and this, I think is, in the main, true."[12] If Moore is right about this, then hedonists have *always* maintained that pleasures-in-context of other properties are alone intrinsically good, and pains-in-context of other properties are alone intrinsically bad. If both "consciousness" and "pleasure" are intentional concepts, then we must always have consciousness-of-pleasure-of-some-specific-kind. Thus, we do seem to be justified in calling our fourth theory "qualitative hedonism."

In one interesting passage in which he discusses "consciousness of pleasure" as the true hedonistic intrinsic good, Moore came very close to seeing that "consciousness" and "pleasure" are both intentional concepts which require objects to be concretely meaningful. He wrote that "it seems quite plain, that we do regard as very desirable, many complicated states of mind in which the consciousness of pleasure is combined with consciousness of other things—states which we call 'enjoyment of' so and so. If this is correct, then it follows that consciousness of pleasure is not the sole good, and that many other states, in which it is included as a part, are much better than it."[13] What Moore never realized, however, was that if pleasure is an intentional concept, there is no way whatsoever to tell that pleasure-in-context is better than pure pleasure in isolation. There is no such thing as pure pleasure in isolation, and it is impossible to "isolate the consciousness of pleasure,"[14] as he repeatedly insists that we must do. The impossibility of thus isolating pure pleasure follows in part from the fact that there is no *one* quality of feeling which we call pleasure, and in part from the fact that *many* of the diverse feelings we desire to sustain and repeat cannot be fully identified or distinguished from one another except in conjunction with other properties.

The Ranking of Pleasures and Pains

How can we tell which specific pleasures are intrinsically better, and which pains are intrinsically worse, than others? In Chapter 2 it was pointed out that the psychological claim that pleasures (and pains) differ in quality is different from the normative claim that differences in quality involve differences in degrees of intrinsic value or disvalue. John Stuart Mill set out to address the psychological question of what it means to say that pleasures and pains differ qualitatively, but actually addressed instead the normative question of how we tell which qualitatively different pleasures or pains are to be preferred to which others. Mill did not deal satisfactorily with the psychological question, though it is hoped that this book is not lacking on this score. He did, however, make some highly plausible suggestions about how to deal with the normative question, to which we are now ready to turn. Mill's suggestion, probably derived from chapter 33 of Plato's *Republic,* or from Book 1, chap. 7 of Hutcheson's *System of Moral Philosophy,* was that a specific kind of pleasure was intrinsically better than another if it was preferred over the other by at least a majority of what we might call "competent rational judges." Though he does not deal quite so specifically with pains, he probably would have accepted the suggestion that a specific kind of pain was intrinsically worse than another if a majority of competent rational judges preferred the latter to the former. By a competent rational judge, Mill seems to have meant a person who satisfies the three conditions of having experienced both sorts of pleasure in question, being talented in introspection and self-knowledge, and being capable of calm, reflective, unprejudiced or disinterested comparison and judgment. We may extract Mill's view of the nature of the competent rational judge and his views on how to identify the "higher" and "lower" pleasures from his *Utilitarianism.*

Of two pleasures, if there be one to which all or almost all who have experience of both give a decided preference, irrespective of a feeling of moral obligation to prefer it, that is the more desirable pleasure. If any one of the two is, by those who are competently acquainted with both, placed so far above the other that they prefer it, even though knowing it to be attended with a greater amount of discontent, and would not resign it for any quantity of the other pleasure which their nature is capable of, we are justified in ascribing to the preferred enjoyment a superiority in quality so far outweighing quantity as to render it, in comparison, of small account.[15]

It is better to be a human being dissatisfied than a pig satisfied; better to be Socrates dissatisfied than a fool satisfied. And if the fool, or the pig, are of a different opinion, it is because they only know their own side of the question. The other party to the comparison knows both sides.[16]

It may be questioned whether any one who has remained equally susceptible to both classes [bodily and mental] of pleasures, ever knowingly and calmly preferred the lower, though many, in all ages, have broken down in an effectual attempt to combine both.

From this verdict of the only competent judges, I apprehend there can be no appeal. On a question which is the best worth having of two pleasures, or which of two modes of existence is the most grateful to the feelings, apart from its moral attributes and from its consequences, the judgment of those who are qualified by knowledge of both, or, if they differ, that of the majority of them, must be admitted as final. And there needs be the less hesitation to accept this judgment respecting the quality of pleasure, since there is no other tribunal to be referred to even on the question of quantity. What means are there of determining which is the acutest of two pains, or the intensest of two pleasurable sensations, except the general suffrage of those who are familiar with both?[17]

According to the greatest happiness principle, as above explained, the ultimate end, with reference to and for the sake of which all other things are desirable—whether we are considering our own good or that of other people—is an existence exempt as far as possible from pain, and as rich as possible in enjoyments, both in point of quantity and quality; the test of quality and the rule for measuring it against quantity being the preference felt by those who, in their opportunities of experience, to which must be added their habits of self-consciousness and self-observation, are best furnished with the means of comparison.[18]

In the initial stages of applying Mill's methods for distinguishing higher and lower pleasures, any two species of pleasure will have to be judged on their own respective merits; but as things progress it might be possible to classify those judged to be superior to others into more general groupings. Whether Mill was right about this or not our modern competent rational judges will have to decide for themselves; but there is no doubt that he thought that the rationally preferred or superior pleasures could all be classified generally as those which were mental and distinctively human. Lower pleasures were generally bodily and of our "animal nature." Unfortunately, Mill did not give a very careful analysis of the distinction between "mental" and "bodily" pleasures; but the suggestion was made in Chapter 2 that "mental" pleasures (or pains) are those given to experience as not having definite bodily locus, and that "physical" pleasures (or pains) as having such a locus. It makes sense to

113

ask where the latter are, but not the former. Mill discusses the intrinsically superior mental pleasures and inferior bodily pleasures in these words:

> But there is no known Epicurean theory of life which does not assign to the pleasures of the intellect, of the feelings and imagination, and of the moral sentiments, a much higher value as pleasures than to those of mere sensation. It must be admitted, however, that utilitarian writers in general have placed the superiority of mental over bodily pleasures chiefly in the greater permanency, safety, uncostliness, etc., of the former—that is, in their circumstantial advantages rather than in their intrinsic nature. And on all these points, utilitarians have fully proved their case, but they might have taken the other and, as it may be called, higher ground with entire consistency. It is quite compatible with the principle of utility to recognize the fact that some kinds of pleasure are more desirable and more valuable than others. It would be absurd that, while, in estimating all other things, quality is considered as well as quantity, the estimation of pleasures should be supposed to depend on quantity alone.[19]

Mill gives very little attention to the question of intrinsically better and worse pains, though Francis Hutcheson had discussed the topic in some detail in the second half of Book 1, chap. 7 of his *System of Moral Philosophy*. Mill does at least suggest a distinction corresponding to higher and lower pleasures. He speaks of the desirability of escaping "the positive evils of life, the great sources of physical and mental suffering—such as indigence, disease, and the unkindness, worthlessness, or premature loss of objects of affection."[20] He does not say explicitly that mental pains are intrinsically worse than physical ones, though he seems to assume it. Certainly many reflective, clear-headed, and impartial people would consider various intense and prolonged localized bodily pains as a lesser evil than equally intense and prolonged psychical nonlocalized despair, depression, fear, terror, anger, hatred, jealousy, loneliness, alienation, boredom, disappointment, grief, or guilt. Bored persons sometimes injure themselves just to break the monotony. Guilt-ridden souls often flagellate themselves just to relieve the guilt. Many dying patients find that they can tolerate great bodily pain once they have resolved such more intolerable pains of soul as guilt, alienation from loved ones, and fear of abandonment as the end comes. Kierkegaard pointed out that the discomfort of intense and prolonged despair was worse than death, for persons possessed by such despair look upon death as a welcome relief.[21] For detailed and profound discussions of the nonlocalized forms of mental suffering, we have to turn to existentialist thinkers such as Kierkegaard, or to modern psychology, rather than to Mill.

It does appear that the "higher" pleasures associated with the various "pluralistic goods" discussed in Chapter 3 are generally of the nonlocalized variety. The agreeable feelings which "accompany" the exercise of freedom of thought, speech, or religion; the joys involved in deep, abiding appreciation of unique friends and loved ones; the enjoyments of beauty in art and in nature; the ecstasies of creativity in art, science, and philosophy; the pleasures of rational inquiry and contemplation; the deep satisfactions of virtuous moral character and activity; even the rapture and blissfulness of the mystic or religious worshiper—none of these pleasures has definite bodily locus, as do the pleasures of sexual orgasm or a back rub or eating a spoonful of sugar. And all these nonlocalized pleasures also satisfy Mill's second criterion of being distinctively human, at least in their more developed forms.

The qualitative hedonist will want to make generalized classifications of superior and inferior pleasures and pains only with great caution. We should understand clearly, however, that if he does conclude that (1) all superior pleasures are nonlocalized, this does not logically commit him to the conclusion that (2) all nonlocalized pleasures are superior. Proposition (2) does not follow from (1) any more than "all pains are feelings" follows from "all feelings are pains." Thus, it would be perfectly consistent with this conclusion of qualitative hedonism if a majority of competent, rational judges classified any of the following nonlocalized pleasures, along with others unmentioned, as inferior pleasures, and most of them even as intrinsic evils: (a) the pleasures of malice, (b) those of sadism or masochism, (c) those of revenge, (d) those of drunkenness or of Huxley's *soma* (assuming that these pleasures are nonlocalized), (e) the pleasant memories of any past localized pleasure, (f) the pleasant memories of any of the pleasures from (a) through (d); (g) enjoyable anticipations of future pleasures from (a) through (e). Even the quantitative hedonist who holds that all intrinsic goods are pleasures—that only pleasures are intrinsic goods—is not *logically* committed to the thesis that all pleasures are intrinsic goods. He may subscribe independently to such a view, as did Aristippus, Epicurus, and Jeremy Bentham, who wrote:

> Let a man's motive be ill-will; call it even malice, envy, cruelty; it is still a kind of pleasure that is his motive: the pleasure he takes at the thought of the pain which he sees, or expects to see, his adversary undergo. Now even this wretched pleasure, taken by itself, is good: it may be faint; it may be short; it must at any rate be impure: yet while it lasts, and before any bad consequences arrive, it is good as any other that is not more intense.[22]

Mill never committed himself to the proposition that "all pleasures are intrinsically good," and I do not regard it as an integral part of qualitative hedonism. Even if it is, the qualitative hedonist could consistently rank pleasures of types (a) through (e) mentioned above, or the pleasures mentioned by Bentham, *very* low qualitatively as well as quantitatively on the scale of positive value. The great instrumental harmfulness of most of them must also be taken into account.

116

Happiness and the Good Life

For both the qualitative and the quantitative hedonist, happiness consists in a positive surplus of pleasure and ideally no pain at all over an extended period of time, and unhappiness consists in a surplus of pain over pleasure and at worst no pleasure at all over an extended period of time. The good life is the happy life and the bad life the unhappy one for both forms of hedonism. But qualitative hedonism introduces significant modifications into the concept of happiness. Not only the amount, but also the quality of pleasure matter, greatly. The qualitative hedonist would not regard the people of Brave New World as happy; for, despite the large amount of pleasure they enjoy, the quality of it is generally inferior because their pleasures are primarily localized ones, and many intrinsically good qualities of pleasure are noticeably lacking.

It should be recognized, however, that qualitative hedonism does not define happiness as consisting *only* in nonlocalized enjoyment, just as it does not define unhappiness as consisting only in nonlocalized suffering. The "lower" pleasures may be inferior intrinsic goods, but they are intrinsic goods all the same. Localized bodily pains may be more tolerable than some of our equally prolonged and intense nonlocalized sufferings, but they are nonetheless intrinsically bad. The hedonistic concept of happiness should provide a complete answer to the question of what is intrinsically good, with nothing worthwhile omitted; and the hedonistic concept of unhappiness should do likewise for what is intrinsically bad, omitting nothing worth avoiding for its own sake. Thus, qualitative hedonism advocates the actualization of *both* inferior and superior pleasures to the extent that they are compatible with one another, just as it advocates the avoidance of *both* localized and nonlocalized suffering to the extent that they can be avoided. When qualitative hedonism says that some pleasures are superior to others, this means that they ought to be chosen in preference to their inferiors when it is impossible to choose both. It does *not* mean that the inferior pleasures are not to be chosen *at all,* only that they are to be avoided when their pursuit interferes with or is incompatible with the actualization of some higher pleasure. Victorian prudery should never be allowed to blind us to their intrinsic importance.

The higher and lower pleasures both have degrees of intrinsic worth, and they can be combined into wholes (not necessarily organic) which have more intrinsic value than either type taken separately. Fortunately, their mutual actualization is often complementary rather than incompatible. Coleridge claimed that tea drinking was "the most intellectual of sensual pleasures."[23] The localized pleasures of a good meal can be combined with the nonlocalized ones of good conversation and companionship to form a total experience of sustained enjoyment which is of greater worth than the good meal all by itself, or the good companionship all by itself, might have been. The localized pleasures of sexual intercourse can be combined with the nonlocalized pleasures of love or intimacy to form a total experience of far greater worth than sex without love, or love without sex, might have been. Since this is the case, if marriage affords us the best of all opportunities for maximizing the actualization of the lower and higher pleasures of sex and intimacy in combination, then a happy marriage will be the best, the most rewarding, of all forms of interpersonal relations. A happy marriage ought to be preferred over loveless sex, no matter the quantity. And it ought to be preferred over any merely "platonic" form of friendship. In a happy marriage, the partners are both friends and lovers, and this is of far more importance than being mere friends, or mere lovers. Thus we have a qualitatively hedonistic justification of a happy marriage.

Pains, also, may be combined with one another to form wholes which are of far greater disvalue than their parts taken separately. It is bad enough to be dying from terminal cancer, and worse to be terrorized by a fear of death; but the combination of the two is far worse than either alone would be. However painful it may be in coming, death with dignity and without fear is to be preferred to death without dignity and with fear. Serious physical suffering often generates black despair over one's condition, and the combination of the two is far worse than physical suffering alone, or dark despair alone.

Happiness is always a matter of degree, but there are differences of quality as well as degrees of quantity. The person who would live the good life must consider both quality and quantity; and he must accept the fact that some periods of life can and will be happier or unhappier than others, partly as a result of factors over which he has little or no control, and partly as a result of factors over which he has a great deal of control. Joyous reflection on these truths can itself be a qualitatively significant part of that happiness.

Action and Obligation

Is it possible to derive a theory of action or obligation from qualitative hedonism as it has been so far presented? As was pointed out in Chapter 1, qualitative hedonism, as such, is an answer to the question "What things are intrinsically good, or bad?" and is not primarily concerned with the questions "What ought we do?" or "How ought we to behave?" We noted that an answer to the question of what is intrinsically good must be given by almost all theories of action, such as egoism, morality, racism, and nationalism. Even deontological moral theories usually recognize a duty to maximize intrinsic goodness as *one* duty among others. In combination with egoism, the hedonistic answer to what is intrinsically good yields the duty to maximize happiness for myself alone. In combination with universalistic morality, it yields the duty to maximize happiness for everyone, or for all sentient beings. This was the form which it took for

119

John Stuart Mill. In combinations with racism or nationalism, it yields the duty to maximize happiness for all the members of my race or nation, and possibly also the corresponding duty to inflict as much suffering as possible upon the members of other races or nations.

It seems possible to combine quantitative hedonism freely with almost any of these theories of action, but this may not be true of qualitative hedonism. Are any of these combinations peculiarly favored by qualitative hedonism, as it has been developed thus far? Has it logical links with one or more of these theories of action which it does not have with others? Epicurus and Bentham, as traditionally interpreted, favored linking their hedonism with egoism; and Mill favored a connection with universalistic morality. Let us explore the question whether qualitative hedonism might have stronger logical links with the latter than with the former by considering the following argument.

(1) Some pleasures are intrinsically superior to others in quality.

(2) Qualitatively superior pleasures ought to be chosen in preference to qualitatively inferior ones, if the latter are incompatible with the former.

(3) The pleasures of prudential virtue and activity are incompatible with the pleasures of moral virtue and activity.

(4) The pleasures of moral virtue and activity are qualitatively superior to the pleasures of prudential virtue and activity.

Therefore, the pleasures of moral virtue and activity ought to be chosen in preference to the pleasures of prudential virtue and activity.

Steps (1) and (2) in this argument have been explained in some detail already, but we need to look more carefully at steps (3) and (4). As for (3), why and how are prudence and morality

incompatible? It is impossible to enjoy simultaneously the pleasures of prudential motivation and activity and the pleasures of
moral motivation and activity because prudence is logically incompatible with morality. The egoistic or prudential point of
view identifies a right act as one that promotes the welfare of
the prudential agent alone, whereas the moral point of view, at
least as understood by universalistic utilitarians, identifies a
right act as one that promotes the welfare of everyone, or at
least the greatest possible number of persons or sentient beings.[24] The former is the ideal of exclusive self-interestedness,
the latter that of universal interestedness. Universalistic
morality makes a place for self-interestedness, without being
egoistic, however. The agent is himself included in the class of
"everyone" or "the greatest number," even where self-sacrifice
is required for the greater good of others. The cost of his
sacrifice to him must be figured in the calculation and balanced
against the gain for others, and the effects of his sacrifice are
counted in, even though he is not made happier by this action.
The important thing is that in a universalistic morality the
agent can have duties to himself and can act to promote his
own interest without becoming an egoist. Here each person,
including oneself, counts as one, and no one as more than one;
yet there is no *exclusive* self-interestedness, as there is in
egoism. It is possible to be self-interested without being exclusively self-interested. But the ideal of promoting the happiness
of the greatest number of persons, oneself included, is logically
incompatible with the ideal of promoting the happiness of oneself alone, even if cooperation with others is seen as a means to
the latter end.

Egoists and moralists may at times choose the same means to
their ends, but the ends are clearly distinct. Enlightened egoists
and moralists may both act on rules that involve telling the
truth, keeping promises, and cooperating with others, as
means to their respective ends. The egoist follows such rules

Pleasures and Pains

because, and to the extent that, they are to his personal long-run advantage; but the moralist follows them because, and to the extent that, they are to the advantage of everyone, or of the greatest possible number. The only egoistic motive is a desire for one's own happiness or welfare, but there are many moral motives, all of which aim at the general welfare, such as a sense of justice, love, kindness, loyalty, sympathy, benevolence, pity, conscientiousness, nobility, and heroism. Even when the egoist cooperates with others, he is *using* them as a means to his own long-range welfare. But when the moralist cooperates with others, he is as much concerned about their welfare as he is about his own. In that sense he treats other people as ends in themselves and never merely as means to his own long-range happiness. It is logically impossible to be exclusively self-interested and at the same time universally interested; thus, egoism and morality cannot be simultaneously enjoyed.

Probably the most controversial premise of our argument is (4). Are the agreeable feelings which "accompany" wanting and acting to promote only one's own welfare qualitatively inferior to those which "accompany" wanting and acting to promote the welfare of everyone? Are the inherent pleasures of the motives and activities of egoism qualitatively inferior to those of the moral motives of justice, love, kindness, loyalty, sympathy, benevolence, pity, conscientiousness, nobility, heroism, and so on, and the activities that regularly issue from these? Our majority of rationally competent judges must finally decide, after experiencing both, and on the basis of cool, careful, clear-headed, disinterested introspective comparison and judgment. *If* the answer is affirmative, then our argument shows that qualitative hedonism does yield a moral theory of motivation and action. We must leave the argument at this hypothetical stage of development; but *if* all four of our premises are true, then qualitative hedonism generates a form of "attitude utilitarianism."[25] Moral virtue is its own reward, in qualitatively hedonistic terms; and we ought to cultivate those attitudes and motives most likely to promote the general welfare of all sentient beings, because the satisfactions inherent in and following from those attitudes and motives are qualitatively superior to the satisfactions of egoism, not to mention those of racism, tribalism, nationalism, and all competing alternatives. If moral virtue is its own reward, this does not mean that the moralist is really an egoist in disguise who seeks reward or intrinsic goodness *only* for himself. A desire for the welfare of another seeks the welfare of that other, even if satisfaction for the agent accompanies its fulfillment.

6

Methodology in Ethics and the Proof of Utilitarianism

In the twentieth century, much attention has been given to the question of methodology in ethics. Where ethics proper attempts to give rationally justified answers to such questions as "What things are good?" and "What acts are right?" the question of what exactly constitutes rational justification belongs to a logically more abstract order of investigation. It is one of the principal questions of metaethics, as opposed to ethics proper. The meaning of such value words as "good," "bad," "right," "wrong," and "ought" is also a principal question of metaethics, although it is not one that will receive much attention here, since our primary concern is with the justification of utilitarianism. We shall ask in this chapter what reason can do to bring about agreement on questions of value and practice. Humans often do disagree heatedly about the good life and what ought to be done to achieve it. What rational methods, if any, are available for resolving such disagreements about the right and the good and other normative issues?

Since critical thinking began, there have always been skeptics who insist that we cannot really reason out our differences on evaluative issues. Many types of philosophical skepticism exist, but we are presently interested in *methodological skepticism,* which maintains that there are no rational methods available for resolving disagreements on questions of value and practice, and which further suggests that there is no hope for any sort of general or universal rational consensus on evaluative issues. Let us take this issue of intersubjective agreement first and then turn to the matter of methodology. Men of reason have always lived by a certain ideal hope, the hope that there exists some set of beliefs about what is, and even about what ought to be, on which all competent rational authorities are ultimately destined to agree. This ideal is not and never has been an actuality, though at times we seem to see degrees of approximation to it. It has deep roots in human psychology. Most of us find something disturbing about confusion, ignorance, misinformation, and disagreement; and reasonable persons have at least seriously entertained the hope that the disturbing characteristics of disagreement are in principle eliminable by reasoning together and thus producing a justified world view about which there is rational consensus.

As opposed to methodological skepticism, *methodological rationalism* insists that rational methods are available, even in the area of value theory, and that such methods make it possible for us to move in the direction of this hoped-for intersubjective rational agreement. The rationalist is not committed to the thesis that we will in fact use these methods; humans may be so perverse, as the theologians insist, that they will never take full advantage of either the rational or the spiritual resources available to them. But this is no refutation of the rationalist. He claims that rational methods are available *if* we will use them, but he is not committed to the claim that we will use them. So much the worse for us and our world, perhaps, if we don't. We may not. Yet the resources are there all the same.

Just as the rationalist is not committed to the claim that we will in fact use the methods available for bringing about a rational consensus in which a unified world view is freely adopted on its own merits through a process of rational reflection, criticism, and persuasion, so the skeptic is not committed to the view that there are no methods at all for bringing about large-scale agreement. It is perfectly compatible with his position to hold that many nonrational techniques of persuasion are available which may be used to bring about such a consensus. Aldous Huxley envisioned a state of universal but nonrational consensus on questions of value and practice in his *Brave New World.* This state was brought about through genetic engineering, prenatal and postnatal conditioning of the most thorough Pavlovian sort, sleep teaching, universal state-controlled and -sponsored drug addiction, complete state censorship and management of the news media, and other such devices. Totalitarian societies often use imprisonment, torture, execution, brainwashing and other such techniques of mind control to bring about consensus in nonrational ways. And in nontotalitarian societies, many nonrational techniques of persuasion flourish, such as advertising, social, religious, political and economic pressures toward conformity, regimented indoctrinations, and revivalism. All of this can be assimilated by the methodological skeptic. His thesis is not that there are no methods at all which can be used to bring about intersubjective agreement, but rather that there are no *rational* methods available for doing so.

The claim that there are no rational methods available in ethics or axiology is often supported by the statement that a radical disanalogy exists between science and mathematics on the one hand, and value theory on the other. Scientists can use "scientific method" to persuade other scientists and even to correct their own past mistakes, and mathematicians can use deductive logic to prove their theorems, but what can the ethicist or axiologist do to support his value judgments? From the obvious gap that exists between "is" and "ought," it is generally inferred that the value theorist can do nothing, but this conclusion may not be as inevitable as it appears on the surface. We may be in a better position to see alternatives to it if we explore some of the methodological similarities and differences between axiology and natural science and mathematics. If the claim that no rational methods are available in axiology is to be refuted, some such methods must be produced, and their applicability to concrete cases must be shown. It is not enough to promise that methods are there without producing any, as philosophers have been known to do. Blank checks cannot be cashed. How can we cash in on the claim that we can reason together to settle our differences on questions of value and practice?

Disagreements in the natural sciences and mathematical disciplines take place on a variety of levels of logical abstraction, and so do disagreements on questions of value and practice. Furthermore, different methodological procedures are appropriate for use at these different levels of abstraction, and the logical level of disagreement must be identified before the usable methodology becomes manifest.

John Stuart Mill insisted that the basic principle of qualitatively hedonistic utilitarianism—that we ought to act to maximize happiness and minimize unhappiness for the greatest possible number of people—could not be proved in one sense of the term "proof," but that it could in another sense. He wrote that "questions of ultimate ends do not admit of proof, in the ordinary acceptation of the term. To be incapable of proof by reasoning is common to all first principles."[1] Mill explained:

> Questions of ultimate ends are not amenable to direct proof. Whatever can be proved to be good must be so by being shown to be a means to something admitted to be good without proof. The

medical art is proved to be good by its conducting to health; but how is it possible to prove that health is good? The art of music is good, for the reason, among others, that it produces pleasure; but what proof is it possible to give that pleasure is good? If, then, it is asserted that there is a comprehensive formula, including all things which are in themselves good, and that whatever else is good is not so as an end but as a means, the formula may be accepted or rejected, but is not a subject of what is commonly understood by proof. We are not, however, to infer that its acceptance or rejection must depend on blind impulse, or arbitrary choice. There is a larger meaning of the word "proof," in which this question is as amenable to it as any other of the disputed questions of philosophy. The subject is within the cognizance of the rational faculty; and neither does that faculty deal with it solely in the way of intuition. Considerations may be presented capable of determining the intellect either to give or withhold its assent to the doctrine; and this is equivalent to proof.[2]

In our discussion of the nature of methodology in ethics, we shall first look very briefly at what Mill might have regarded as ordinary reasoning, then turn to the more interesting and important question of proving axioms or first principles by what he called some "larger meaning of the word 'proof.'" Ordinary reasoning is useful in ethics, though at levels less abstract than that of first principles. We shall illustrate our discussion of ordinary proof by considering subordinate questions of value and practice of special interest to hedonists, both quantitative and qualitative.

Ordinary Evidential Methods of Reason

The first two levels of methodology in ethics, which we shall discuss in this section, would have been regarded as reason "in the ordinary acceptation" by Mill. Levels three through five, to be discussed later, will present reason as it functions in the adoption of axioms or first principles.

Methodology in Ethics and the Proof of Utilitarianism

(1) *Observation, inductive inference, and "scientific method"* can be used at a certain level to solve disagreement on questions of value and practice, though these methods have limitations which we shall soon explore. Getting at the relevant facts is one way of positioning ourselves for making a rational judgment or decision on such questions. In actual practice, we often disagree on what is right or what is best or what ought to be done because we disagree about the facts that have a bearing upon the cases at hand, and we can settle disagreements of this kind by getting the facts straight through processes of observation, inductive inferences, and the sorts of methodological moves which generally parade under the label of "scientific method." If scientific methodology can be used anywhere, it can be used in axiology, and it is just as available here as anywhere else. Facts do have some sort of bearing on what we ought to do and on what is best for us. This is a simple matter of common sense and everyday practice. Let us see how the process works. We want to know whether entities actually have the characteristics that they ideally ought to have. If we live in a technologically primitive culture situated in a warm climate, we may find that we frequently become seriously ill after eating pork. We may then begin to wonder whether we ought to eat pork, and if we are reasonably intelligent we will decide on good grounds that we ought not to do so. We may eventually establish strict taboos against it. It is a matter of knowing what causes what in the world, in this case that eating rotten pork causes serious illness or even death, but foodstuffs ideally ought not to do that. Of course, we presuppose the value judgment that serious illness and death are undesirable, but this may be safely assumed at certain logical levels of disagreement. If our technology changes, and refrigeration is invented, then a different set of facts will have a bearing on the question of whether we ought to eat pork, and our decision could be otherwise, all other things being equal.

129

Questions about means to ends are factual questions, and there is a great deal of room for disagreement among hedonists as to the most efficient means for actualizing pleasure or happiness, hedonistically conceived. What makes a person happy? What makes him "have fun" or "enjoy himself" or "feel good" over an extended period of time? In answering, hedonists may draw up different and debatable lists of "instrumental goods," that is, things which typically cause or produce sustained agreeable feeling; and such lists may include advice about how to avoid pain as well as how to pursue happiness. Some hedonists such as Epicurus have offered rather austere regimens for pursuing happiness. Epicurus did not recommend a life of wine, women, song, gourmet tastes, and general debauchery, as we often mistakenly assume. History seems to have remembered that he recommended the pursuit of pleasure, but forgotten his views on how to get and sustain it,[3] and overlooked passages in which he apparently identified pleasure with a neutral state of feeling in which there is no pain rather than with a positive state of agreeable feeling. As for the *means* to happiness, Epicurus recommended a life of almost monastic simplicity—a diet of bread and water, with an occasional piece of cheese when a person really wants to have a blast, the cultivation of a few like-minded friends, civil obedience and harmony, the development of the kind of practical and philosophical knowledge which bestows freedom from irrational fears, and preferably no sex or physically entangling alliances, though sex was not altogether forbidden. But other hedonists have doubted that the Epicurean way is indeed the most efficient means to the end of maximizing pleasure and minimizing pain over the long run. They hold, in light of more adequate factual information, that a varied diet that prevents malnutritional diseases is essential to life and health, to say nothing of happiness; that although not everyone is dispositionally suited for the quiet contemplative life, people are not thereby made ineligible to run the race for happiness; that with all their pains, jealousies, and liabilities laid bare, sex and family life offer adequate compensation, and so on.

Unfortunately, the desirability or undesirability of known consequences is not something that follows simply from a mere factual acquaintance with the consequences themselves. Facts must be measured by an ideal standard of excellence. Factual information totally separated from all evaluative standards is irrelevant to value theory, and such information becomes relevant only when a background of evaluation is given or assumed, just as observations become relevant in natural science only when a background of theory is given or assumed. The "bare facts" are of no scientific significance whatsoever; they become scientifically interesting only when they are plugged into some theoretical system which interprets and interrelates them. Similarly the "bare facts" are of no significance to ethics; they become ethically interesting only when they are plugged into an ethical system which interprets and interrelates them. If the would-be heroin user really wants to be the kind of man that heroin will transform him into, he will not be rationally dissuaded from taking heroin by having his attention called to the causal connections involved; and if the would-be eater of rotten pork really wants to be ill or even dead, he will not be rationally dissuaded by the bare facts from eating it.

Thus, the methods of observation, inductive inference, and scientific experimentation cannot be the only rational methods available for use in axiology or in science. Some techniques for introducing an evaluative framework for appraising the facts and a theoretical framework for organizing the scientific data must be employed. Some way of arguing about the appropriateness of the values and the theories must be available, and we shall now turn to that issue.

(2) *Deductive reasoning* can be helpful at certain levels of disagreement on questions of value and practice. Natural science

and mathematics have no monopoly on deductive logic. If it is useful anywhere in arriving at rational agreement, it is also useful in the area of axiology. For example, it may be used to show the logical incompatibility of certain value judgments, thus forcing the rejection of at least one of them; or it may be used to infer a more concrete norm from a more abstract norm, thus giving a good reason for accepting the former. These uses of deduction illustrate but do not exhaust its possibilities. As Mill well knew, there are limitations to the application of deductive procedures, but they are encountered in all intellectual disciplines which utilize deduction and are not peculiar to ethics or axiology.

Not only do we make value judgments, but we can and often do have reasons for making them. We can even formalize the matter and cast these reasons into the molds of deductive logic. Even where it is not done in fact, it nevertheless could be done. Both the uses and the limits of deductive argumentation in ethics may be illustrated by the three following arguments:

Argument A: Acts of stealing are *prima facie* wrong.
This act is an act of stealing.
Therefore, this act is *prima facie* wrong.

Argument B: If any kind of act usually results in needless suffering, then acts of that kind are *prima facie* wrong.
Acts of stealing usually result in needless suffering.
Consequently, acts of stealing are *prima facie* wrong.

Argument C: If we could not will that everyone in similar circumstances should perform acts of a certain kind, then acts of that kind are wrong.
We could not will that everyone in similar circumstances should perform acts of stealing.
Thus, acts of stealing are wrong.

Note that the first normative premise in Argument A appears as the conclusion of Argument B and may be supported by that line of argumentation. A more absolutistic version of this conclusion appears in Argument C and may be deduced from its premises. The line of argumentation expressed in Argument B is essentially utilitarian, and that expressed in Argument C is essentially deontological or Kantian. The first premise of Argument C is a version of Kant's categorical imperative, statable as "Always act on that maxim which you could will to become a universal law." We need not decide here which is the best way to support the conclusion that "acts of stealing are wrong." We do see that it can be supported through rational deductive argumentation, but what are the limits of this procedure? Each new argument seems to require still other arguments to support *its* premises; and to get a normative conclusion, each of these new arguments must have at least one controversial normative premise. How far can this process of providing proofs for proofs for proofs be extended? It can be extended *indefinitely, but not infinitely.* This implies that somewhere at the end of the process a normative judgment must be accepted without argumentative proof. Mill called such fundamental norms "axioms" or "first principles." Let us call them *ultimate norms,* norms which in a given value system are so fundamental logically that they cannot be derived from other norms more fundamental than themselves. Such norms will be highly abstract, and may define a complete way of life. As far as their "surface grammar" is concerned, some of these ultimate norms may not look like norms; they may be presented as definitions, as "self-evident truths," as axioms of "pure reason," as generalizations about "human nature," or as pseudostatistical reports about "normalcy." But in their "depth grammar," these ultimate premises are normative in function, in the sense that they set an ideal standard, which more than likely is a controversial one; and they are simply accepted within a given scheme of thought without further proof. Jeremy Bentham had such ultimate norms in mind when he said that "that which is used to prove everything else, cannot itself be proved; a chain of proofs must have their commencement somewhere."[4] Kant's categorical imperative and Mill's principle of utilitarianism have been historically important examples of such ultimate norms, as have been the hedonistic judgment that only happiness is intrinsically good and the pluralistic judgment that other things besides happiness are intrinsically good.

Must such ultimate norms be "arbitrarily accepted," or is there something more that men of reason can do in practice to arrive rationally at agreement? Whatever this "something else" is, it cannot be "ordinary" in nature, since all ordinary argumentative and evidence-giving procedures are included at methodological levels 1 and 2. Mill suggested that there was still something left for reason to do, even after all such ordinary argumentative methods have been exhausted. What "larger meaning of the word 'proof'" is it possible to give?

The Larger Meaning of "Proof"

Many philosophers would say, no doubt, that it is true especially at the level of ultimate norms that our values must be "arbitrarily chosen." This is where our methodological skeptic may be allowed to have another inning, for he may admit that observation and inductive and deductive reasoning may be used in axiology in the ways we have explored thus far, while still maintaining that at the level of *ultimate* norms there is nothing left for reason to do but make an arbitrary choice of standards.

If we are going to meet the objections of the methodological skeptic, we must first examine the notion of "arbitrary." It may be suspected that many of those who claim that values must be chosen arbitrarily do not have a clear notion of the meaning or meanings of the term—in other words, that they do not really know what they are talking about. The notion of "arbitrary" takes whatever meaning it has from the opposite notion of "rational," and the word "arbitrary" is used arbitrarily unless it is accompanied by a clear concept of what the opposite "nonarbitrary" alternative consists in. Usually, "nonarbitrary" just means "rational," and where the "nonarbitrary" or rational is conceived to be the logically inferential, then the arbitrary is that which is not logically inferential or logically inferred. In this sense of "arbitrary," the ultimate norms of value are indeed arbitrary, but so are all other paradigms of rationality such as the axioms of mathematics, geometry, and logic, the principle of the uniformity of nature which underlies all scientific and inductive reasoning, and all the basic principles of all human knowledge whatsoever. In this sense, value theory is just as arbitrary as, but no more arbitrary than, all the rest of human knowledge. Actually, this is a fairly innocent sense of "arbitrary," for it means only that all human knowledge has to begin somewhere with a certain set of assumptions, to which there may be specifiable alternatives. It means that deductive reasoning can proceed only a finite number of steps up the ladder of abstraction, and that in a finite number of operations we must arrive at that principle which is used to prove all else, but which cannot itself be proved in the sense of being logically derived from something more fundamental than itself.

Admitting all this, we can still ask meaningfully whether it is reasonable to adopt some given set of ultimate assumptions. This query shifts the problem of justification away from the assumptions themselves and toward the act of adopting them. It also brings a different sense of "reasonable" and "arbitrary" into play. Here "reasonable" does not mean "logically inferred from some set of evidential premises," and "arbitrary" does not mean "not logically inferred from evidential premises." There is more to reasonableness than logical inference and argument, whether they be of the deductive or the inductive type. Logic is the core of rationality, but it is not the sum total of it. There is a difference between a rational choice of values and an arbitrary choice of values, even after all the arguments and evidential premises have been accounted for. A man of reason can make and will want to make more moves after all the argumentative tools of rationality have been exhausted. What are some of these trans-argumentative methods of reason which can be used to justify the act of adopting ultimate norms or first principles in ethics?

(3) *Rational intuition* has been offered by some philosophers as a trans-argumentative rational method for justifying the adopting of ultimate norms. When rational intuition comes into play, ultimate axioms of knowledge are simply given and immediately recognized as "self-evidently true" by all rational beings, without evidential proof. This method is rejected by most contemporary thinkers, primarily on the grounds that what seems self-evident to one person or in one culture may be contradicted by what seems self-evident to another person or in another culture. It is always possible to defend intuitionism by saying that where conflicting intuitions appear, rational intuition is just not functioning properly in at least one of these cases. But specifying just how the proper functioning of rational intuition is to be recognized as such and distinguished from its opposite is indeed difficult.

In the first chapter of his *Utilitarianism,*[5] and in his *Autobiography* and other works, Mill repeatedly attacked and rejected rational intuitionism. In his *Autobiography* he called it "the German, or *a priori* view of human knowledge, and of the knowing faculties,"[6] and commented:

> The notion that truths external to the mind may be known by intuition or consciousness, independently of observation and experience, is, I am persuaded, in these times, the great intellectual

support of false doctrines and bad institutions. By the aid of this theory, every inveterate belief and every intense feeling, of which the origin is not remembered, is enabled to dispense with the obligation of justifying itself by reason, and is erected into its own all-sufficient voucher and justification. There never was such an instrument devised for consecrating all deep-seated prejudices.[7]

Thus, when Mill speaks of some "larger meaning of the word 'proof,'" he clearly does not have intuitionism in mind. We shall follow him in rejecting this as a legitimate method of reason in ethics. Then what did Mill have in mind by the "larger meaning"? He seems to have intended two things, the first of which has proved historically to be as infamous as the rationalistic appeal to self-evident truths. He seems to have meant both deriving ethical first principles from non-normative premises, and appealing to the rational preferences of competent rational judges.

(4) *Deriving ultimate norms from non-normative premises* has been a highly suspect extra-ordinary argumentative procedure in ethics since David Hume pointed out the difficulties in inferring an "ought" from an "is." Yet the oldest attempts to "prove" hedonism seem to have involved the attempt to infer the hedonistic ideal of life from factual assumptions about human nature. Aristotle tells us that Eudoxus, who was a contemporary of Plato and a member of Plato's Academy, "thought pleasure was the good because he saw all things, both rational and irrational, aiming at it."[8] Epicurus followed the same line of reasoning; Diogenes Laertius tells us that "as proof that pleasure is the end he points out that all living creatures as soon as they are born take delight in pleasure, but resist pain by a natural impulse apart from reason."[9] Such considerations at best might show that pleasure is *a* good, but not that it is the *only* good, as the hedonist contends. And they still leave a gap to be bridged between the factual and the normative.

Pleasures and Pains

In confronting us with his "larger sense of 'proof,'" Mill seems to have had in mind primarily some process of deriving his normative principle of utilitarianism from certain factual claims about human nature. The axiom or ultimate norm of qualitatively hedonistic utilitarianism was that "we ought to act to maximize happiness or minimize unhappiness for the greatest possible number of sentient beings." Now, this principle is analyzable into two distinct components, a qualitatively hedonistic answer to the question of what is intrinsically good and bad, and a universalistically moral answer to the question of how we ought to act. The principle of utilitarianism is thus two ultimate norms combined into one, a theory of intrinsic goodness and a theory of action or obligation. Mill's infamous deduction of "the principle of utility" from the alleged necessities of human psychology, which we shall now examine, is offered by him as a "proof" of the first principle that only happiness is intrinsically good. We shall later see how he attempts to tie this in with the claim that we ought to act to maximize happiness and minimize unhappiness for all sentient beings.

Mill attempted to deduce the normative claim that only happiness (as understood by his own *qualitative* hedonism) is intrinsically good from certain non-normative premises drawn from the realm of psychology. Those who jump immediately to the conclusion that such "proofs" cannot succeed, since normative conclusions cannot be derived from non-normative premises, should at least reflect upon the fact that the reverse procedure of justifying non-normative assumptions by appealing to normative considerations is often regarded as quite acceptable in philosophical disputation. It is usually agreed that the axioms of geometry, logic, and arithmetic, for example, along with the principle of the uniformity of nature upon which all scientific reasoning rests, cannot be proved, without circularity, using reason "in the ordinary acceptation of the term." We cannot, without circularity, give a geometrical proof for the axioms of geometry, as we can for its derived theorems, or a logical proof for the axioms of logic, as we can for its derived theorems, or a scientific proof for the assumption of the uniformity of nature, as we can for the derived theorems of scientific knowledge. However, it is often maintained that we can give a *pragmatic* justification for the adoption of these fundamentals of human knowledge. Now, a pragmatic justification is a derivation of non-normative principles from normative ones. We conclude that we are justified in adopting the axioms of geometry, logic, science, and so on from the premises that these are means to our ends and that the ends (such as knowing the world and predicting and controlling events) are desirable. In a pragmatic justification, normative judgments about the desirability of ends provide good reasons for adoption of non-normative premises.

Now, Mill's "proof" of the claim that only happiness is desirable for its own sake, or intrinsically good, is just the reverse of pragmatic justification. It involves justifying the adoption of a normative judgment on the basis of a non-normative judgment, but we shall see that a normative premise is presupposed by the argument. Mill argued that we should accept the normative conclusion that only happiness is desirable as an end in itself on the basis of the psychological premise that happiness is the only thing that anyone is ever capable of desiring as an end. As Mill put it, "to desire anything except in proportion as the idea of it is pleasant, is a physical and metaphysical impossibility."[10] He needlessly complicated his argument for the desirability of happiness by drawing an unfortunate analogy between "desirability" and "visibility," which has irked his critics considerably:[11]

The only proof capable of being given that an object is visible is that people actually see it. The only proof that a sound is audible is that people hear it; and so of the other sources of our experience. In like manner, I apprehend, the sole evidence it is possible to produce that anything is desirable is that people do actually desire it. If the end which the utilitarian doctrine proposes to itself were not, in theory and in practice, acknowledged to be an end, nothing could ever convince any person that it was so.[12]

Now, there is a real difference between "capable of being desired" and "ought to be desired," that is, is desirable; and Mill's argument by analogy shows us only that happiness is capable of being desired, not that it ought to be desired, and not that it *alone* ought to be desired. Mill further argues that it alone is in fact desired for its own sake, maintaining that all other things are desired as means to happiness or, as in the case of virtue, health, power, and money, as *a part* of happiness. As we found in Chapter 5, the claim that these things are a part of happiness is not "contemptible nonsense" if we understand what Mill meant by this. He meant that the possession of these things is itself inherently enjoyable, that "to each of these there is a certain amount of immediate pleasure annexed,"[13] and that they are desired only because they are inherently enjoyable. We maintained in Chapter 5 that competent rational judges would find that other things, totally divorced from all satisfaction, are not desirable. Mill tries to show, however, that happiness alone is desirable for its own sake by first establishing the factual premise that happiness alone is desired for its own sake. But a commitment to some form of pluralism does not seem to be psychologically impossible, and even if we grant Mill's questionable psychological premise, a gap remains to be bridged between the "is" and the "ought." This can be partially achieved by introducing one more premise into the argument, which Mill may have been implicitly assuming. His argument thus far, with the new premise added, may be summarized as:

(1) Happiness is desired for its own sake.

(2) We cannot desire anything for its own sake other than happiness.

(3) If we are obligated to do something, then we can do it.

Deductions:

(4) If we cannot do something, then we are not obligated to do it. (3) Transposition.

(5) If we cannot desire anything for its own sake other than happiness, then we are not obligated to do it. (4) Universal Instantiation.

(6) We are not obligated to desire anything other than happiness for its own sake. (5), (2) Modus Ponens.

With the introduction of the "ought implies can" principle, premise 3, we can then move logically to the conclusion, step 6, that nothing other than happiness ought to be desired for its own sake. This does not of itself establish the positive conclusion that happiness ought to be desired, for its own sake, that it is desirable; but it does rule out all the competition. Eliminating all the competition is a significant step in the philosophical justification of any position; and maybe there is another rational method, such as the appeal to the rational preference of competent rational judges, which can be used to establish the positive conclusion. If Mill was assuming the "ought implies can" principle, and if it is true that we are capable of desiring only happiness as an end, then he was not being as stupid as his critics assume, at least in narrowing down the possibilities to one. He wrote: "If the opinion which I have now stated is psychologically true—if human nature is so constituted as to desire nothing which is not either a part of happiness or a means of happiness, we can have no other proof, and we require no other, that these are the only things desirable."[14]

Is the "ought implies can" principle a normative principle? If so, then Mill, if he made use of it, was still deriving norms from norms rather than from purely non-normative assumptions. It does appear to be normative, "cannot implies not obligated" being equivalent in meaning to "it is wrong to hold a person obligated to do something when he cannot do it."[15] Also, some systems of value apparently do not make use of it; so there are alternatives to it.[16] If we take it to be somehow ultimate or fundamental as a norm, the question arises as to how reason might justify its adoption, and an attempt to answer will take us into a discussion of still other non-argumentative rational methods in ethics. But first we must look at Mill's proof of universalistic morality.

As we have seen, utilitarianism is a theory of action as well as an answer to the question of what is intrinsically good. Does Mill attempt to justify the axiomatic assumption that we ought to act to maximize happiness and minimize unhappiness for all sentient beings? Yes, he has an argument, though his critics have been as unkind to it as they have to his proof that happiness alone is intrinsically good or desirable for its own sake. Mill argued, "No reason can be given why the general happiness is desirable, except that each person, so far as he believes it to be attainable, desires his own happiness. This, however, being a fact, we have not only all the proof which the case admits of, but all which it is possible to require, that happiness is a good; that each person's happiness is a good to that person, and the general happiness, therefore, a good to the aggregate of all persons."[17]

The usual criticism is that Mill here commits the informal logical fallacy of composition, the fallacy of reasoning that a certain whole has a certain property because each of its parts has that property. The fallacious argument is that the "general happiness" is desirable because the happiness of each person is desirable, or that each person desires the "general happiness" as an end because he desires his own happiness as an end.

We must grant that Mill does not fully explain what he is doing here, but it is possible to give a different and more sympathetic interpretation. Instead of uttering egregious nonsense, Mill might have been anticipating what R. M. Hare has called the "universalizability" feature of language. Both descriptive and normative language incorporate a rule which says that if we ascribe a given predicate to something, we are logically committed to ascribing that predicate to anything which is like it in relevant respects. As Hare puts it, "If I call a thing red, I am committed to calling anything else like it red. And if I call a thing a good X, I am committed to calling any X like it good."[18] Mill could very well be trying to tell us that if we call happiness good in our own case, we are committed by such a universalizability rule of language to calling happiness good in *all* cases. Granted, he does not make explicit appeal to such a linguistic rule; but we could introduce it as a way of making sense of his move from regarding one person's happiness as good to regarding the happiness of all persons as good. Mill at least does say that the principle of utility "is a mere form of words without rational signification unless one person's happiness, supposed equal in degree (with the proper allowance made for kind), is counted for exactly as much as another's,"[19] and that it can be "correctly described as supposing that equal amounts of happiness are equally desirable, whether felt by the same or different persons."[20]

The universalizability rule of language is still a normative linguistic principle. It tells us what we *ought to* do with words. If it must be introduced to make sense of moving from the goodness of the happiness of one to the goodness of the happiness of all, we are not yet inferring normative conclusions from *purely* non-normative considerations. If happiness as such is intrinsically good, and if it is our duty to maximize intrinsic good, then it is as much our duty to maximize it for other sentient beings as for ourselves. This assumes, of course, that the fact that the happiness is *mine* is not a relevant consideration.

(5) *Appealing to the rational preference of competent rational judges* is the other trans-argumentative rational method that Mill uses

in ethics. He employs it, as we noted, to distinguish between the "higher" and the "lower" pleasures. He does not explicitly use it in justifying the adoption of his "greatest happiness" principle. We have seen that this principle is analyzable into an ultimate normative answer to the question of what is intrinsically good—namely, happiness in the qualitatively hedonistic sense—and an ultimate normative answer to the question of how we ought to act—namely, to promote the greatest happiness of the greatest possible number of people or sentient beings. Now, Mill *could* have and *should* have appealed to the deepest rational preferences of rationally competent judges to justify the adoption of both of these ultimately normative or axiomatic features of his ethics. If he had done so, he might have been on much firmer ground than he was in trying to justify them on the basis of purely non-normative premises, which never quite seems to work. In Chapter 5 we saw that a rationally competent judge had to satisfy the three conditions of having experienced both of two competing values, being talented in introspection and self-knowledge, and being capable of calm, reflective, unprejudiced or disinterested comparison and judgment. Let us suppose now that instead of having to decide the respective merits of two or more qualitatively different pleasures or pains, our competent rational judges are required to consider the axiomatic hedonistic and pluralistic answers to the question of what is intrinsically good or bad, or the egoistic versus the universalistically moral theory of action or obligation. If a decisive majority of our competent rational judges found that they preferred a qualitatively hedonistic theory of intrinsic goodness, combined with a universalistically moral theory of action or obligation,[21] what better justification for our ultimate ethical norms could we ask for?

The appeal to the deepest rational preferences of competent judges suggested by Mill definitely anticipated the non-argumentative methods of *vindication* and *rational choice* developed in recent years by Paul Taylor as a means of justifying the adoption of those ultimate principles of value which define for us a given way of life. These two methods tend to merge, in practice, into each other, and both of them appeal finally to the rational preferences of persons who have done their best to satisfy those conditions which must be satisfied if such rational preferences are to come to the surface. Such preferences are for experienced ways of life, not for self-evident propositions, though they may themselves receive a propositional expression.

The method of vindication[22] involves asking a person—yourself or another—who is in a cool, calm, reflective, clear-headed state, such questions as: What do you really want out of life? What kind of world do you really want to live in, or pass on to your children and grandchildren? On the surface, such a procedure might seem impotent for the task of minimizing our disagreement with others on questions of value and practice, but it really is not impotent at all. One reason we disagree is surely that we have not taken time out from the business of coping with day-to-day existence to consider such questions. If we did give such matters more thought, it is highly probable that we would move closer together in our values and principles of action. Earth Day, for example, is a practical implementation of this method. The intent here is to provide us with an opportunity to reflect in a cool, calm, clear-headed manner on the question of what kind of physical environment we want for ourselves and for posterity. Our treatment of *Brave New World* in Chapter 3 may also be viewed as an application of this method to the hedonism-pluralism controversy.

The method of rational choice[23] is an extension of the method of vindication, in a sense. It comes into play in axiology when we are at the level of those ultimate norms or first principles that define for us a given way of life. It involves our choosing a way of life as defined by our ultimate norms under a certain set of conditions, which are just the opposite of the conditions of "arbitrary choice." A rational choice of a way of life as defined by our ultimate norms involves identifying our deepest preferences in values and practices after we have done our best to meet the conditions of freedom, enlightenment, and impartiality that such a choice requires. An arbitrary choice, by contrast, is made under conditions of unfreedom, ignorance, and bias or prejudice. As an absolute ideal, rational choice is unattainable by any human being, but there are significant degrees of approximation to it which we mere mortals can make. The effective use of the method of rational choice or preference presupposes that we have adequately employed the argumentative, evidence-giving procedures discussed at levels 1 and 2 earlier in this chapter. It presupposes that we have at our disposal all the relevant facts, and that we have fully explored all the logical ramifications, implications, and applications of all the alternative styles of life being considered.

Freedom here does not mean the absence of all conceivable restraints, but rather of certain particular restraints that make rationality, broadly understood, impossible. It involves the ideal absence of external constraints, such as lack of opportunity, monolithic social conditioning, the threat of imprisonment, torture, brainwashing, financial ruin, social rejection, and so on, and also of such internal restraints as *overwhelming* desire, appetite, passion, emotion—though not of *all* desire, appetite, passion, and emotion, as the Stoics might have preferred. It involves the ideal absence even of unconscious powers, motives, or constraints over which we have no voluntary control. This condition is hard to satisfy completely, but not all our beliefs and values (including the belief that all our beliefs and values are determined by the unconscious) can be determined by our unconscious, and the main point of psychotherapy seems to be to bring our unconscious problems up to the level of conscious awareness so that we can cope with them at that level. In other words, the main purpose of psychotherapy is to contribute to our freedom from domination by unconscious powers and motives.

Incidentally, without using the word "freedom" in this context, Mill recognized that freedom, in the sense just presented, was necessary for the proper functioning of the method of rational preference. He maintained that a majority of (unfree) men might opt for the lower as opposed to the higher pleasures.

> Capacity for the nobler feelings is in most natures a very tender plant, easily killed, not only by hostile influences, but by mere want of sustenance; and in the majority of young persons it speedily dies away if the occupations to which their position in life has devoted them, and the society into which it has thrown them, are not favorable to keeping that higher capacity in exercise. Men lose their high aspirations as they lose their intellectual tastes, because they have not time or opportunity for indulging them; and they addict themselves to inferior pleasures, not because they deliberately prefer them, but because they are either the only ones to which they have access, or the only ones which they are any longer capable of enjoying.[24]

Enlightenment is the second requirement of rational choice. Mill insisted that a competent rational judge of values had to have knowledge of the alternatives being considered, preferably by direct experiential acquaintance. Paul Taylor also requires that a rational choice of those values and principles which constitute a given way or ideal of life be made under conditions of knowledge rather than under those of ignorance. Taylor recognizes the importance of intellectual and imaginative knowledge, as well as the sort of direct experiential knowledge emphasized by Mill.[25] We can intellectually understand the principles which define for us a given way of life, as well as their logical implications. We often must settle for an imaginative projection of ourselves into a given life-style, such as that of *Brave New World*. But we may also know what our own deepest rational preferences are from the experience of having actually lived in accord with a variety of ideals of life.

According to Taylor, what we ought to know about a given way of life includes (a) the nature of the values and principles that define it, (b) its cost, (c) its consequences, and (d) all the alternatives to it. Mill insisted that "it is a preliminary condition of rational acceptance or rejection that the [utilitarian] formula should be correctly understood."[26] This could be said of any formula or set of formulas that constitute the first principles of a given ideal of life. Not only must we understand one alternative; ideally all the others would be fully explored. The citizens of *Brave New World* who were exposed to only one possible way of life never could have made an enlightened choice of values.

Impartiality, or freedom from bias and prejudice, functions in philosophy as a rational virtue and within morality proper as a moral virtue. As a rational virtue it requires that we play fairly and justly with ideas and ideals, and in morality it requires that we play fairly and justly with persons or sentient beings.[27] As a rational virtue, impartiality requires that we give the alternative ideals of life which we confront a fair hearing, without having made up our minds in advance. A rational choice of any given way of life or social order requires that we prefer it without knowing in advance what our social position or status in that order will be.

Impartiality or disinterestedness should never be confused with uninterestedness. The impartial courtroom judge is not uninterested in the case before him, and the impartial rational judge is not uninterested in the ideas and ideals which come before him. Impartiality is actually a special kind of deep interestedness, a deep concern for fair play in the arena of competition among ideas and ideals.

In his defense of freedom of thought and discussion in his essay *On Liberty,* Mill insisted that a free impartial exchange of opposing and critical ideas is necessary for the cultivation of the rational understanding. Even if certain people are commonly regarded as "educated men," if they have not been exposed to such a free exchange of ideas respecting "moral and human subjects," they are still not in a position properly to judge the grounds of their own opinions. "He who knows only his own side of the case," Mill wrote, "knows little of that."[28] Such one-sided, closed-minded persons do not even understand their own beliefs. "All that part of the truth which turns the scale, and decides the judgment of a completely informed mind, they are strangers to; nor is it ever really known, but to those who have attended equally and impartially to both sides, and endeavored to see the reasons of both in the strongest light."[29]

Without appealing to the rational intuition of a "self-evident truth," both Mill and Taylor have presented us with a rational method for arriving at and justifying our commitment to those first principles or ultimate norms that define our chosen way of life. First principles in ethics which define for us a given way of life and give our deepest rational preferences a conceptual expression do not have to be arbitrarily chosen, in the sense of being selected under conditions of compulsion and restraint, or ignorance, or prejudice. They can be rationally chosen. Rationality, as involving freedom, enlightenment, and impartiality, is an achievement and not an innate natural inheritance of "rational animals." There are many degrees of approximation to these conditions of rationality, but the more we approximate to these conditions, the better we *can* decide whether happiness, understood in qualitatively hedonistic terms, is an intrinsic good, and perhaps the only intrinsic good, for ourselves and for all sentient beings. If a majority of competent rational judges share this belief with us, then we have the best of reasons for being qualitatively hedonistic utilitarians. But if our majority of competent rational judges should reject this belief, then we would have the best of reasons for abandoning it. Either way, we will give intersubjective validity to our values.

As a final observation, it might be worth noting that Mill did not make exorbitant claims for his method of appeal to the preferences of rationally competent judges. He expected, at best, *majority* consensus to result from the application of this method. This was a majority of rational persons who had made every effort to use available rational methods, not merely a majority of persons as such, including those who had made no serious effort to reason out their values. But Mill seemed to leave room at the top for minority dissent. Perhaps this is the most, also, that we should claim for Paul Taylor's closely related methods of vindication and rational choice. It seems possible to satisfy the requirements of rationality, yet to differ in our deepest preferences from the majority of others who also satisfy the requirements of rationality. At this level, having done all else, we simply have to agree to disagree.

Notes

1. What Is Hedonism?

1. It is sometimes said that the hedonist is committed to a fourth claim that *all* pleasure is intrinsically good, and *all* pain is intrinsically bad. I shall maintain in Chapter 5 that the qualitative hedonist is not committed to this thesis. I shall also explain later that it is the conscious *experience* of pleasure, and not simple (unconscious) pleasure, which is alone intrinsically good for the hedonist.

2. *The Portable Nietzsche,* Walter Kaufmann, ed. (New York: Viking, 1954), p. 468.

3. Moore developed his concept of the "naturalistic fallacy" primarily in chapter 1 of his *Principia Ethica* (Cambridge: Cambridge University Press, 1959).

4. *Utilitarianism, with Critical Essays,* Samuel Gorovitz, ed. (Indianapolis: Bobbs-Merrill, 1971), p. 22.

5. Ibid., p. 21.

6. Bentham's egoism is more clearly expressed in his *Deontology* than it is in his *Principles of Morals and Legislation.* However, Bentham was at best only a co-author of the *Deontology,* most of which was written by John Bowring. For a discussion of whether Bentham wrote or fully committed himself to the *Deontology,* see *Collected Works of John*

Stuart Mill, J. M. Robson, ed. (Toronto: University of Toronto Press, and London: Routledge & Kegan Paul, 1969), Vol. 10, pp. xxxvi and 520.

7. John B. Watson, the father of modern behavioristic psychology, published in 1928 his *Battle of Behaviorism: An Exposition and an Exposure,* in which he advanced the metaphysical thesis that consciousness does not exist. Metaphysical behaviorism is to be distinguished from a weaker methodological behaviorism that merely denies the accessibility of consciousness to "legitimate" sensory methods of investigation.

2. Do Pleasures Differ Qualitatively?

1. *Utilitarianism, with Critical Essays,* Samuel Gorovitz, ed. (Indianapolis: Bobbs-Merrill, 1971), p. 19.

2. C. D. Broad, *Five Types of Ethical Theory* (London: Routledge & Kegan Paul; New York: Humanities Press, 1956), p. 232.

3. Brand Blanshard, *Reason and Goodness* (London: George Allen & Unwin, 1961), p. 311.

4. *The Works of Jeremy Bentham,* John Bowring, ed. (New York: Russell & Russell, 1962), Vol. 2, p. 253.

5. John Hospers, *Human Conduct: An Introduction to the Problems of Ethics* (New York: Harcourt Brace Jovanovich, 1961), p. 58.

6. Henry Sidgwick, *The Methods of Ethics* (London: Macmillan, 1901), p. 94.

7. Hospers, *Human Conduct,* p. 112.

8. Gilbert Ryle, *Dilemmas* (Cambridge: Cambridge University Press, 1960), p. 58.

9. Hospers, *Human Conduct,* p. 112.

10. Ibid., pp. 111–112.

11. Ibid., p. 113.

12. Ibid.

13. Ibid.

14. Rollo May, *Love and Will* (New York: Dell, 1969), p. 150.

15. Hospers, *Human Conduct,* p. 59.

16. The qualitative hedonist at least recognizes differences in kind between pleasures. I would include instances of both types of pleasure in a hedonistic definition of "happiness," while maintaining that one type is more important or essential than the other. More about this in Chapter 5.

17. Hospers, *Human Conduct,* p. 113.

18. Ibid., p. 116.

19. Ibid., p. 112.
20. The intentionality of some pleasure and pain concepts is explained in Chapter 4, and the precise relation between "sources" and "objects" of intentional pleasures and pains is further clarified.

3. *A Critique of Quantitative Hedonism*

1. Aldous Huxley, *Brave New World and Brave New World Revisited* (New York: Harper & Row, 1965), pp. xx, xxi. The whole of *Brave New World Revisited* develops this theme in detail.
2. Ibid., p. 169.
3. Ibid., pp. 182-183.
4. Ibid., p. 170.
5. Ibid., p. 42.
6. Ibid., p. 169.
7. J. J. C. Smart and Bernard Williams, *Utilitarianism, For and Against* (Cambridge: Cambridge University Press, 1973), p. 19.
8. Ibid., p. 22.
9. Ibid., pp. 20-21.
10. Ibid., p. 22.
11. The information given in this paragraph is a summary of findings reported in Robert G. Heath, "Electrical Self-stimulation of the Brain in Man," *American Journal of Psychiatry*, 120 (1963), 571-577. Copyright 1963. Other relevant articles are: M. P. Bishop, S. Thomas Elder, and Robert G. Heath, "Intracranial Self-Stimulation in Man," *Science*, 140 (1963), 394-396; Robert G. Heath, Stanley B. John, and Charles J. Fontana, "The Pleasure Response: Studies by Stereotaxic Techniques in Patients," in *Computers and Electronic Devices in Psychiatry*, Nathan S. Kline and Eugene Laska, eds. (New York and London: Grune & Stratton, 1968), pp. 178-189; Robert G. Heath, "Pleasure and Brain Activity in Man," *The Journal of Nervous and Mental Disease*, 154 (1972), 3-18.
12. Francis Hutcheson, *A System of Moral Philosophy* (New York; Augustus M. Kelley, 1968), Vol. 1, pp. 117-118.
13. Ibid., pp. 118-119.

4. *A Systematic Exposition of Qualitative Hedonism*

1. See Book 10, chaps. 4 and 5 of Aristotle's *Nicomachean Ethics*, reprinted in *The Basic Works of Aristotle*, Richard McKeon, ed. (New York: Random House, 1941), pp. 1098-1102.

2. Ibid., p. 1104.

3. Ibid., p. 945.

4. Joseph Butler, *Fifteen Sermons Preached at the Rolls Chapel* (London: G. Bell & Sons, 1914), Sermon 3, p. 66.

5. *Utilitarianism, with Critical Essays*, Samuel Gorovitz, ed. (Indianapolis: Bobbs-Merrill, 1971), p. 32.

6. Ibid., p. 34.

7. Ibid., p. 38.

8. Ibid.

9. G. E. Moore, *Principia Ethica* (Cambridge: Cambridge University Press, 1959), p. 72.

10. *Utilitarianism*, p. 18.

11. Ibid., p. 39.

12. Ibid., p. 40.

13. *The Stoic and Epicurean Philosophers*, Whitney J. Oates, ed. (New York: Modern Library, 1940), p. 41.

14. Mill's position has been defended in various ways in: Dorothy Mitchell, "Mill's Theory of Value," *Theoria*, 36 (1970), 100–115; Rex Martin, "A Defence of Mill's Qualitative Hedonism," *Philosophy*, 47 (1972), 140–151; and Henry R. West, "Mill's Qualitative Hedonism," *Philosophy*, 51 (1976), 97–101.

15. Moore, *Principia Ethica*, pp. 12–13.

16. Ibid., p. 13.

17. Ibid., p. 78.

18. *The Dialogues of Plato*, B. Jowett, trans. (New York: Random House, 1937), Vol. 2, pp. 344–345.

19. Moore, *Principia Ethica*, p. 80.

20. I discuss "desire" as an intentional concept in some detail in my *Freedom, Responsibility and Obligation* (The Hague: Martinus Nijhoff, 1969), pp. 5–10.

21. There is a brief history of the concept of intentionality, and an exploration of its psychological significance in Rollo May, *Love and Will* (New York: Dell, 1969), chaps. 9 and 10. For a recent philosophical discussion, see Roderick Chisholm, "Intentionality and the Mental," in *Minnesota Studies in the Philosophy of Science* (Minneapolis: University of Minnesota Press, 1958), Vol. 2, pp. 524 ff. See also Richard E. Aquila, *Intentionality: A Study of Mental Acts* (University Park, Pa.: The Pennsylvania State University Press, 1977).

22. This point is discussed in connection with the concept of "desire" in my *Freedom, Responsibility and Obligation*, pp. 5–10.

23. C. D. Broad, *Five Types of Ethical Theory* (London: Routledge & Kegan Paul, 1956), p. 235.
24. *Nic. Eth., Basic Works of Aristotle*, p. 1097.
25. Ibid., p. 1100.
26. *The Chief Works of Benedict De Spinoza*, R. H. M. Elwes, trans. (New York: Dover, 1951), Vol. 2, p. 168.
27. John Hospers, *Human Conduct: An Introduction to the Problems of Ethics* (New York: Harcourt Brace Jovanovich, 1961), p. 69.
28. *Dialogues of Plato*, Vol. 1, p. 556.
29. Ibid., Vol. 2, pp. 44, 378.
30. Broad, *Five Types of Ethical Theory*, pp. 188-189.
31. *Dialogues of Plato*, Vol. 1, p. 843.

5. *Some Unanswered Questions*

1. G. E. Moore, *Principia Ethica* (Cambridge: Cambridge University Press, 1959), p. 62.
2. Ibid., pp. 188-189.
3. Ibid., p. 184.
4. Ibid., pp. 83-84.
5. Ibid., pp. 84-85.
6. As presented, for example, in John Hospers, *Human Conduct: An Introduction to the Problems of Ethics* (New York: Harcourt Brace Jovanovich, 1961), chap. 3, pp. 121-138.
7. *The Dialogues of Plato*, B. Jowett, trans. (New York: Random House, 1937), Vol. 2, pp. 352-354.
8. Brand Blanshard, *Reason and Goodness* (London: George Allen & Unwin, 1961), p. 301.
9. William K. Frankena, *Ethics* (Englewood Cliffs, N.J.: Prentice-Hall, 1963), p. 74.
10. G. E. Moore, *Ethics* (London: Oxford University Press, 1958), pp. 153-154.
11. Hastings Rashdall, *The Theory of Good and Evil* (London: Oxford University Press, 1938), Vol. 1, pp. 153-154.
12. Moore, *Principia Ethica*, p. 90.
13. Ibid., pp. 95-96.
14. Ibid., p. 95.
15. *Utilitarianism, with Critical Essays*, Samuel Gorovitz, ed. (Indianapolis: Bobbs-Merrill, 1971), p. 19.
16. Ibid., p. 20.

17. Ibid.
18. Ibid., p. 21.
19. Ibid., pp. 18–19.
20. Ibid., p. 23.
21. See *Fear and Trembling* and *The Sickness unto Death* by Sören Kierkegaard, trans. Walter Lowrie (Princeton, N.J.: Princeton University Press, 1941), Princeton Paperback #129, p. 145.
22. Jeremy Bentham, *An Introduction to the Principles of Morals and Legislation* (Oxford: Clarendon, 1876), chap. 10, p. 102n.
23. Rashdall, *Theory of Good and Evil*, Vol. 1, p. 16n.
24. I realize fully that this is a controversial definition of the moral point of view, but I choose to use it anyway. Its defense requires another book.
25. Attitude utilitarianism has been developed by Michael Scriven, *Primary Philosophy* (New York: McGraw-Hill, 1966), chap. 7. Scriven's argument for it is quite different from the one given here, however.

6. *Methodology in Ethics and the Proof of Utilitarianism*

1. *Utilitarianism, with Critical Essays,* Samuel Gorovitz, ed. (Indianapolis: Bobbs-Merrill, 1971), p. 37.
2. Ibid., p. 15.
3. John Hospers is particularly good on this topic. See his *Human Conduct: An Introduction to the Problems of Ethics* (New York: Harcourt Brace Jovanovich, 1961), pp. 49–52.
4. Jeremy Bentham, *An Introduction to the Principles of Morals and Legislation* (Oxford: Clarendon, 1876), chap. 1, p. 4.
5. Mill also rejected the appeal to "moral sense" in chapter 1 of his *Utilitarianism,* but I do not discuss moral sense, since the objection of cultural variability applies equally to it.
6. John Stuart Mill, *Autobiography of John Stuart Mill* (New York: Columbia University Press, 1969), p. 157.
7. Ibid., p. 158.
8. *Nicomachean Ethics, The Basic Works of Aristotle,* Richard McKeon, ed. (New York: Random House, 1941), p. 1094.
9. "The Life of Epicurus," *The Stoic and Epicurean Philosophers,* Whitney J. Oates, ed. (New York: Random House, 1940), p. 63.
10. *Utilitarianism,* p. 40.
11. See G. E. Moore, *Principia Ethica* (Cambridge: Cambridge University Press, 1959), pp. 66–67. There is a fine defense of Mill's

"proof" against Moore's critique in Everett W. Hall, "The 'Proof' of Utility in Bentham and Mill," *Ethics,* 60 (1949), 1–18.

12. *Utilitarianism,* p. 37.

13. Ibid., pp. 38–39.

14. Ibid., pp. 39–40.

15. The normative features of "ought implies can" are explored in my *Freedom, Responsibility and Obligation* (The Hague: Martinus Nijhoff, 1969), pp. 105–106.

16. Ibid., pp. 84–85, 103–104.

17. *Utilitarianism,* p. 37.

18. R. M. Hare, *Freedom and Reason* (Oxford: Clarendon, 1963), p. 15.

19. *Utilitarianism,* p. 55.

20. Ibid., p. 56n. In a letter written in 1868, Mill explained that "when I said that the general happiness is a good to the aggregate of all persons I did not mean that every human being's happiness is a good to every other human being; though I think, in a good state of society and education it would be so. I merely meant in this particular sentence to argue that, since A's happiness is a good, B's a good, C's a good, etc., the sum of all these goods must be a good." See *Collected Works of John Stuart Mill,* Francis E. Mineka and Dwight N. Lindley, eds. (Toronto: University of Toronto Press, and London: Routledge & Kegan Paul, 1972), Vol. 16, p. 1414.

21. The theory of action involved here could take the form of either act utilitarianism or rule utilitarianism. This, too, in the final analysis, is a matter of rational preference. Mill's own position on this controversy is unclear. The act utilitarian holds that that individual act is right which is likely to have the best consequences for everyone. The rule utilitarian holds that a concrete rule of behavior is justified if everyone's acting upon it would have the best consequences for everyone, and that an individual act is right if it falls under a justified rule. Philosophers are still debating the question whether the distinction between act and rule utilitarianism is viable. Both forms must answer the question: What things are intrinsically good? This book has been addressed primarily to this question.

An act utilitarian application of my theory of qualitative hedonism to the field of medical ethics has been developed by my student Bonnie Voigtlander, in her doctoral dissertation completed at the University of Tennessee in 1978 entitled "An Ethical Theory for Medical Decision Making with Special Reference to Neonatal Intensive Care."

22. Paul W. Taylor, *Normative Discourse* (Englewood Cliffs, N.J.: Prentice-Hall, 1961), p. 132.

23. Ibid., chap. 6.

24. *Utilitarianism*, p. 20.

25. Taylor, *Normative Discourse*, pp. 166–170.

26. *Utilitarianism*, p. 15.

27. Failure to make this distinction between rational and moral virtue resulted in my erroneous attempt to identify rationality and morality in my article "On Being 'Rational' about Norms," *The Southern Journal of Philosophy*, 5 (1967), 180–186.

28. *The Philosophy of John Stuart Mill*, Marshall Cohen, ed. (New York: Random House, 1961), p. 227.

29. Ibid., p. 228.

Index

159

Index

Index

Pleasures and Pains

Designed by Richard E. Rosenbaum.
Composed by The Composing Room of Michigan, Inc.
in 10 point Baskerville V.I.P., 3 points leaded,
with display lines in Baskerville.
Printed offset by Thomson/Shore, Inc. on
Warren's Number 66 Antique Offset, 50 pound basis.
Bound by John H. Dekker & Sons, Inc.
in Holliston book cloth
and stamped in All Purpose foil.

Library of Congress Cataloging in Publication Data
(For library cataloging purposes only)

Edwards, Rem Blanchard.
  Pleasures and pains.

  Includes bibliographical references and index.
  1. Hedonism. I. Title.
BJ1491.E36   171'.4   79-4168
  ISBN 0-8014-1241-2